Non-Profits with Hard Hats

Building Affordable Housing

Non-Profits
with
Hard Hats

Building Affordable Housing

Christine Kuehn Kelly

Donald C. Kelly

Ed Marciniak

National Center for Urban Ethnic Affairs
Washington, D.C.

Cover design by Susan Atlas Kelley. Photographs by Bruce S. Edwards (p.104), Virginia Marciniak (pp.41,92), Boston Moody (p.74), Linda Stevens (p.54) and Harry Tun (p.31).

Contents

Foreword

The dream of safe, decent and affordable housing for all American families was first advanced in the U.S. Housing Act of 1937. This law, a major commitment by the federal government, was enacted not just to help combat the Depression, but also to extend homeownership, create a federal mortgage insurance program and spur the development of rental apartments for a growing population.

For fifty years the national commitment to housing has transformed that dream into reality for the majority of American families. Through the Federal Housing Administration's insurance programs, 52 million families have been afforded the security of owning a home of their own. Through the VA Home Loan Guaranty Program, 12 million more families have gained that right. Federal programs for rental housing have sheltered another 4 million families. Yet millions more stand outside the door, their dreams unfulfilled because they lack income or a down payment. It is no secret, then, that U.S. housing initiatives must be strengthened further to reach those at the low to moderate end of the income scale.

This incisive study of housing ventures by non-profit organizations adds another dimension to this characteristically American story. Ed Marciniak is one of the most provocative thinkers about urban life in the United States today. He and his co-authors, Christine Kuehn Kelly and Donald C. Kelly, explore how local non-profit housing sponsors and community organizations have become important builders of this dream, holding unlimited potential to house families and strengthen America's neighborhoods. In six case studies, *Non-Profits with Hard Hats* details with vibrant color how forward-thinking sponsors met difficult market challenges to provide more affordable housing to low and moderate income families in a variety of neighborhood settings. What is remarkable about these initiatives is that they became the turning points in diverting neighborhoods away from precipitous decline. In fact, these efforts most often served as an early sign that a neighborhood seeking self-improvement could succeed. Where such an enterprising group does not exist, neighborhood livability indeed becomes a formidable task.

Non-Profits with Hard Hats does the nation a favor. It documents and analyzes, in vivid history, six housing experiments within a city noted for inventing social institutions--from Hull House to Saul Alinsky's community organizations scaled to be the building blocks of cities. Chicago is indeed a city of neighborhoods. Without question, Chicago's neighborhoods have been the laboratories that often inspired the development of social institutions successfully adopted later by the rest of America.

A debt of gratitude is in order to Chicago, to the book's three authors, and most of all to the six neighborhood-based organizations. They are the true pioneers of the 21st century. Most importantly, all shape a fresh consensus for future public policy in housing and urban revitalization. We welcome the future they prescribe.

> Marcy Kaptur
> Member of Congress
> 9th District, Ohio

Chicago: The Six Housing Sites

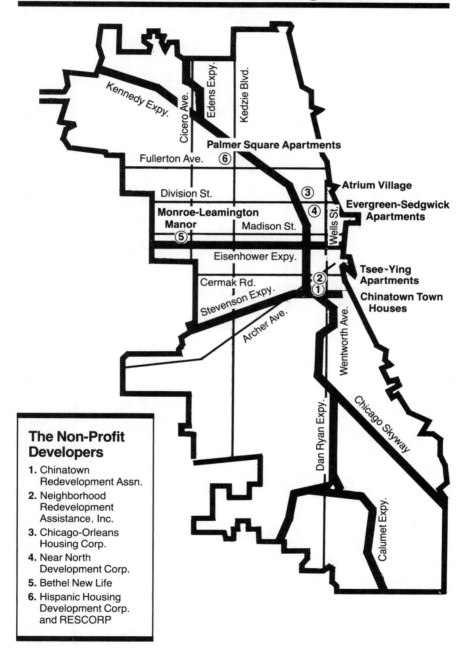

Palmer Square Apartments

Fullerton Ave. ⑥

Division St. ③ — Atrium Village

④ — Evergreen-Sedgwick Apartments

Monroe-Leamington Manor

Madison St.

⑤

Eisenhower Expy.

Cermak Rd.

② — Tsee-Ying Apartments

① — Chinatown Town Houses

Kennedy Expy.

Cicero Ave.

Edens Expy.

Kedzie Blvd.

Wells St.

Stevenson Expy.

Archer Ave.

Wentworth Ave.

Dan Ryan Expy.

Chicago Skyway

Calumet Expy.

The Non-Profit Developers

1. Chinatown Redevelopment Assn.
2. Neighborhood Redevelopment Assistance, Inc.
3. Chicago-Orleans Housing Corp.
4. Near North Development Corp.
5. Bethel New Life
6. Hispanic Housing Development Corp. and RESCORP

9

1

Why Non-Profits
Reached for Hard Hats

During the 1970s and 1980s many of Chicago's lower-income families discovered a new resource to satisfy their housing needs. It was the increasing supply of housing units built or rehabilitated by private, not-for-profit, housing developers. Previously, households with low or moderate incomes had two basic choices: privately owned housing, which they could ill afford, or public housing owned and operated by the Chicago Housing Authority (CHA), a government agency.

The new urban reality is that each year a larger proportion of Chicago's stock of housing for lower-income families is produced by community-based, not-for-profit organizations. This local trend is also nationwide. The Bureau of National Affairs' *Housing & Development Reporter* noted that "small non-profit entities that can undertake rehabilitation and construction...are replacing larger developers," because they can produce housing "more efficiently and with less overhead."[1]

Initiatives That Worked

The six case studies that follow introduce the general public to noteworthy initiatives taken by not-for-profit sponsors to make good housing more affordable and more available to residents in Chicago's older neighborhoods. In each case the housing development became part of an overall strategy for neighborhood revitalization. In several cases housing sponsors were able to cushion the impact of racial and ethnic change upon their neighborhood, simultaneously accommodating newcomers and older residents.

What is the explanation for the new housing roles adopted by not-for-profit organizations in Chicago? Why does their share of the housing market for households in inner-city communities keep growing steadily? Five trends prompted not-for-profit developers to step in and show what they could do to augment the dwindling supply of safe and sanitary housing.

In the first place, not-for-profit groups discovered, through personal experience, that they could become catalysts for neighborhood renewal by intervening in a local housing market shunned by conventional lenders and developers. The six not-for-profit sponsors, whose enterprises are recounted here, not only took risks which a for-profit developer was unwilling to assume but could also attract public and private resources, such as grants and special subsidies, available only to not-for-profit sponsors. Such successful housing developments gave their inner-city neighborhoods a vote of confidence, thus compelling for-profit developers, insurance companies and investors to take a second look at neighborhoods which they had been bypassing. The housing initiative of a not-for-profit sponsor released the market forces necessary to spur neighborhood revitalization.

Soaring Housing Prices

In the second place, nationwide housing trends in the 1980s, conspicuously on display in Chicago, reduced the supply of housing which families of low and moderate incomes could afford to buy or rent. In the private sector, the cost of new residential construction and the rehabilitation of existing apartments--those without any city, state or federal subsidy--skyrocketed. Thus the price of the new housing for sale or rent soared beyond the reach of most lower-income families. Even many of the privately owned apartments, built partially with federal subsidies, asked rents too expensive for families located at the lower rungs of the income ladder. The renting of affordable, privately owned apartments which are not substandard was increasingly seen by many households as an elusive objective.

Thirdly, in many sections of Chicago, such as the Uptown, Edgewater, Kenwood, Garfield Park and Austin communities, hundreds of housing units in multi-family apartment buildings stand vacant. Boarded-up and no longer available for rent, many of these multi-family buildings were actually abandoned by their owners. Each year such buildings continue to be demolished. Between 1970 and 1980, more housing units in Chicago were destroyed than built; 61,274 units were demolished during this decade, while only 50,343 new units were constructed. Between 1980 and 1987, 27,605 housing units were demolished, while 28,577 new units were built.[2] Such massive demolition depleted a desperately needed supply of rental housing for lower-income households. In these two decades, the housing torn down, in the main, had once been occupied by families with low to moderate incomes. But the new construction was predominantly for residents with middle to upper incomes.

Demolishing Good Buildings

The State of the Chicago Region, a report card made public in 1987 and sponsored by seven public and private bodies (Chicago Association of Commerce and Industry, Chicago United, City of Chicago's Department of Planning, Civic Committee of the Commercial Club, Illinois State Chamber of Commerce, Metropolitan Planning Council and the Northeastern Illinois Planning Commission), concluded:

> Abandonment of modestly priced housing units has taken place at an alarming rate, with over 61,000 homes and apartments lost between 1970 and 1980 in Chicago.

> This abandonment and demolition has taken its toll on many Chicago neighborhoods, where windowless buildings and empty lots impart a feeling of hopelessness and discourage new investment. Because of high construction costs, new housing built in the city does little to offset loss of affordable housing. Much of the city's new housing construction and rehabilitation has taken place in a few desirable communities, where housing is an investment as well as shelter....

> Chicago is facing a major problem of housing affordability. There is increasing disparity between the costs of building, rehabilitating and operating housing and the ability of citizens to pay the rental and ownership costs to live in decent housing. The visible results of this problem are the abandonment and demolition of buildings that are no longer economically viable, leaving a legacy of neighborhood deterioration and decay, and the increasing number of homeless people who crowd the few public shelters on cold winter nights. Less visible are the fifth of the Chicago families who pay more than half of their incomes in rent, leaving little for food, clothing or medical care, and those living in overcrowded or substandard apartments.[3]

City Hall's best kept secret is the actual number of these vacant residential properties in Chicago, from single-family houses to large, multi-family apartment buildings. It has been estimated that 35,000 housing units were vacant, boarded-up and delinquent in their real estate taxes at any given time during the 1980s. It is public knowledge that 4,000 to 6,000 of these housing units are demolished each year. The buildings which are now vacant or which are likely to become vacant in the near future offer the city its single best opportunity to house tens of thousands of families with low and moderate incomes. Since the buildings stand empty, their rehabilitation requires no displacement of residents. Chicago desperately needs a local "Marshall Plan" to halt further abandonment of multi-family properties and to save those that are already vacant by rehabilitating them and renting the renovated apartments to families of low and moderate incomes. Putting these buildings back on the tax rolls would ease the tax burden that is now borne by the city's property owners.

Declining Federal Role

Fourthly, federal funds to expand the nation's supply of government-owned public housing or to construct privately owned apartments for lower income families were drastically cut back during the 1970s and 1980s. For example, the annual spending by the federal Department of Housing and Urban Development for low-income housing in Illinois dropped from $286 million in 1984 to $34 million in 1987, an eighty-seven percent decline.[4] Such cuts in the federal housing budget not only reflected a desire to slash the national debt but also the United States Congress' conviction that the U.S. public housing program nationwide was in serious trouble and that new ways would have to be found to provide safe and decent housing for the urban poor. In a special report, "Building from the Bottom Up," the editors of *Time* magazine found that:

> From Boston and Chicago to San Francisco, non-profit development corporations, civic-minded church groups, foundations and companies have stepped into the vacuum left by the federal government's withdrawal from large-scale public housing construction....

> Convinced that such outlays are wasteful, the President has slashed housing aid and abruptly halted new construction, promoting instead a market-driven approach to the problem. Com-

munity groups are quick to note that they cannot solve the housing shortage without renewed help from the federal government. Yet by developing more efficient construction techniques and innovative financing, the smaller builders hope to pioneer new solutions that draw on both public and private resources. As these groups demonstrate "more frugal ways, more effective ways to house the poor," observes [real estate] developer James Rouse, "we can emerge with federal programs that will make much more sense and will encourage enterprise and resourcefulness."

The key to the private group's success is getting local communities involved, which clears away expensive and time-consuming political obstacles to projects.[4]

In 1967 the State of Illinois, through the Illinois Housing Development Authority, began to play an important role in expanding the state's supply of housing for lower-income families by providing additional housing dollars. Using federal housing subsidy programs in conjunction with its own financing capability, the IHDA had by 1987 generated more than 30,000 new and rehabilitated dwelling units throughout the state for families of low and moderate incomes, for the elderly and for the handicapped. Seventy-five percent of these housing units were subsidized. In addition, public/private housing partnerships were organized in Chicago through the joint use of funds from the City of Chicago's department of housing and local private corporations.

Government-owned Slums

Fifthly, the number of families with children living in public housing in Chicago has been decreasing since 1970. While the demand for apartments by low-income families kept growing, the Chicago Housing Authority's actual share of this residential market declined. Even though the stock of CHA-owned family units increased during this period, the number of such apartments actually available for rent declined by more than 5,000. This increase did not occur overnight. How did it happen?

In the tallest high rises, many of the top floors are no longer being rented. (In the nineteen-story buildings of the Cabrini-Green public housing project, for example, the top four floors are sealed off. They were deemed unsafe and undesirable for occupancy by families with children.) Five vacant, fifteen-story buildings (a sixth partially occupied), owned by the CHA, stand

ominously along the lakefront on Chicago's south side; they are
now patrolled by around-the-clock security guards. Elsewhere,
vandalized apartments or those in need of major repairs remain
empty, awaiting renovation or demolition. Hundreds of CHA-
owned apartments are being used for non-residential purposes,
such as offices, police stations or day care centers. Many more
of the CHA apartments built for families with children are being
occupied by adults only. And vacancies continue to multiply in
all large, high-rise projects for families.

Increasingly, low-income families eligible for public housing
display reluctance to move into the city's giant, high-rise public
housing projects which are now called, euphemistically, "the
troubled projects." As a CHA staff person noted, "The applicants for family units are not dummies. They know which projects have the worst reputations." The "official" count of CHA
residents dropped from 137,000 in 1970 to approximately
95,000 in 1984, a thirty-one percent decrease. In Cabrini-Green
Homes, according to CHA's own statistics, the resident population dropped from 17,535 in 1970 to 8,684 in 1984, a fifty percent drop. In Robert Taylor Homes, the number of residents declined from 27,000 in 1970 to 15,000 in 1984, a forty-three
percent decline.

A New Neighborhood Presence

For these five reasons, the arrival of not-for-profit corporations in Chicago's housing market during the 1970s and 1980s
came as a welcome surprise. New developers of more affordable
housing had to be found. Neighborhoods had to be revitalized.
Lending institutions had to be persuaded to take a second look at
inner-city neighborhoods which had been "redlined." New ways
had to be found to preserve the existing stock of multi-family
apartment buildings. Housing alternatives had to be found for
families trapped in giant, high-rise public housing projects. Finally, not-for-profit, community-based developers of housing
would be especially sensitive to the needs of residents who had
to be displaced.

From where did these not-for-profit corporations come?
They were, in the main, grassroots initiatives from inner-city
communities. In such deteriorating neighborhoods, community
groups, church institutions and local leaders established not-for-
profit housing groups to build anew or to rehabilitate moderately
priced housing, so that residents in search of apartments could

remain in the neighborhood. There was an additional challenge whenever religious institutions saw their mission as serving the housing needs of their members or neighbors. Such indigenous institutions were also ready to customize the housing to the needs of neighborhood residents. According to the Chicago Rehab Network, more than 10,000 housing units are currently managed by community-based, not-for-profits in Chicago.

Stimulating Neighborhood Revitalization

These not-for-profit institutions and their leaders saw, as one of the reasons for the decline of their neighborhoods, the lack of involvement by the for-profit sector (banks and other lenders, developers, and insurance companies). Through the vehicle of a not-for-profit housing corporation, these institutions learned that they could build or rehabilitate where the for-profit sector could not or would not. The success of such initiatives then made it attractive for private investors, insurers and builders to return. In this way both institution and neighborhood were conserved.

The case studies in this report describe the efforts of six not-for-profit developers to provide more affordable housing in Chicago's inner-city neighborhoods and to stimulate their revitalization. The obstacles that had to be overcome and pitfalls that were adroitly avoided are summarized in the final chapter.

Selected from a much more comprehensive list of not-for-profit housing developers, the six not-for-profit sponsors were chosen because the housing they built met the following criteria:

• planned to be primarily residential;

• provided housing at more affordable, below-market prices;

• entailed new construction or substantial rehabilitation;

• located within the City of Chicago;

• embraced sixteen or more units;

• used innovative methods or development techniques which could be replicated elsewhere; and

• demonstrated a track record of five or more years of successful operation.

The case studies turned out be be six short stories, some with dramatic episodes, about the Chinatown Town Houses and the Tsee-Ying Apartments for the elderly, located in the Chinatown neighborhood; the Evergreen-Sedgwick Apartments and Atrium Village in the Near North Side community; Monroe-Leamington Manor in the Austin community; and Palmer Square Apartments in the Logan Square community.

These studies are primarily narratives, not technical analyses. They focus on the not-for-profit developer's goals, experience and subsequent reflections; on the obstacles encountered and overcome; on methods used to make the housing more affordable; and on lessons to be shared with other not-for-profit organizations who are considering the sponsorship of a housing development of their own. Furthermore, each housing development is situated within the context of neighborhood revitalization.

The Six Case Studies

While each developer may have perceived his or her obstacles as unique, they were, in fact, common barriers which a not-for-profit sponsor would likely confront in any inner-city neighborhood. In their pursuit of more affordable housing, these community-based and not-for-profit developers demonstrated ingenuity, displayed resourcefulness and showed sensitivity to the needs of their local communities. Hence, the six case studies will prove instructive to housing practitioners elsewhere in Chicago and other urban centers throughout the nation.

There are, at the present time in Chicago, nearly 100 not-for-profit sponsors of housing. In all, they own and manage thousands of units. Many have gone through experiences similar to those recounted in the six case studies and have proved to be equally successful. Their accomplishments, unfortunately, could not be chronicled here. Our hope is that this report will encourage them to tell their own stories as well.

Our inspiration to undertake the six housing case studies came from the pathfinding work of housing entrepreneur Gung-Hsing Wang. His early initiatives in Chinatown spurred local leaders in other Chicago communities to venture on their own and to build on his experience. When they ran into obstacles, many turned to Wang for counsel and encouragement.

NOTES

1.   As quoted in the Summer 1987 newsletter published by The Partnership Institute of the Howard University School of Business and Public Administration, Washington, D.C.

2.   Jan Crawford, "Wrecking ball cuts housing for poor," *Chicago Tribune,* November 29, 1987.

3.   *The State of the Region: Policy Issues and Options for the Chicago Metropolitan Area* (January 1987), a report from the Regional Partnership's Regional Agenda Project.

4.   Robert A. Slayton, "The Reagan Approach to Housing: An Examination of Local Impact," a report of the Chicago Urban League, November 1987.

5.   *Time*, February 9, 1987, pp. 22-23.

2

The Town Houses
of Chinatown

*We planted a seed, to generate neighborhood
confidence in the viability of Chinatown. I
think it has taken root.*--Gung-Hsing Wang

Chinatown, a neighborhood on the near south side of Chicago, found itself at a crossroads in the early 1960s. At that time this small, quiet community had approximately 4,000 residents, eighty percent of whom were Chinese, the remainder mostly Italian. Chinatown's future was uncertain. Why? The pressure of a growing Chinese population, due to immigration, and the decreasing availability of land, due to highway construction, were forcing an exodus of upwardly mobile Chinese unable to locate housing to their liking in Chinatown but who could find such housing elsewhere in the city or suburbs.

Increasingly, those who remained were those compelled to live in Chinatown due to financial or ethnic constraints: owners of local businesses, the elderly, the financially deprived, those who could not speak English. The steady departure of Chinatown's middle class took its toll on the local business sector, precipitating further neighborhood decline.

The residents of Chicago's Chinese community were a quiet people inured by culture to self-discipline rather than complaint. By circumstance they were of limited means. And until recent decades they had been designated by law as second class citizens. Under such conditions they could easily be shoved aside by more aggressive interests. How then would Chinatown proceed with the revitalization of its neighborhood? Who would provide the leadership?

The Historic Setting

In 1870 T.C. Moy, a Chinese merchant from San Francisco, set up a medicine shop and grocery at the south end of Chicago's central business district. He encouraged other Chinese from California to settle nearby, so that by 1890 they numbered about 500. Most of them were laborers with little or no formal education, and because of language and cultural barriers, it was almost impossible for them to find employment, except as domestic help. Their alternative was to become self-employed, principally in restaurants, laundries or specialty stores.

As the central business district prospered and expanded, the modest Chinese community was soon threatened by higher land prices and high-rise developments. Chinese businesses were displaced. A decision was made by leading Chinese merchants to migrate to a new location. By 1907 the move was well underway to an area two miles to the south of the original settlement. The migration became "official" when the On Leong Businessmen's Association also relocated there.

Here, the actions of government stunted the orderly expansion of the new Chinatown at Wentworth Avenue and 22nd Street (renamed Cermak Road as a memorial to Chicago Mayor Anton Cermak who was assassinated in 1933). In 1933 the widening of Cermak Road for the Chicago World's Fair eliminated nearly half of the community's housing stock. The more devastating development, however, occurred in the 1950s when the State of Illinois built two interstate expressways encircling the community and biting off additional housing in the process. So compliant was the image of the Chinese community that the State had no qualms about taking even more property for an expressway extension known as the "Franklin Connector," which it never bothered to build. During this era clout, Chicago style, was obviously not part of Chinatown's neighborhood ethos.

The Immigrant Poor

By 1959 the Chinese community had grown to nearly 4,000 residents. Many were immigrants who had arrived in the United States after the relaxation of immigration laws in 1943. For most, the language and culture of their new land remained a barrier;

they usually found employment as low-paid waiters or laundry workers. The average family income was low. In 1959 half of Chinatown's households lived below the poverty line, then set at an annual income below $2,973.

Restrictive U.S. immigration laws had contributed negatively to the Chinese self-image. From 1882 to 1943 the Chinese had been excluded *by law* from becoming American citizens.[1] Such official discrimination left a residual effect upon the Chinese-American psyche, even after the laws were liberalized in 1943 during the presidency of Franklin D. Roosevelt. The public style of Chinese-Americans had become, or so it seemed, subservient, inconspicuous and passive.

Another cultural characteristic played a role as well, a trait which would ultimately supply the bootstrap by which the Chinese community would lift its fortunes. It was the quality of self-reliance. Chinese-Americans rarely looked to government to solve their problems. That would be an embarrassment. Better to suffer poverty than to ask for public aid. Better to live in substandard housing than to live in a public housing project owned and managed by the government.

The Threat from City Hall

The Chinese-American community in Chicago hoped that such a stance would be respected so that if they asked for nothing, they would be left alone. But the dominant Western culture did not understand or respect such humbleness. The silence of Chinese-Americans continued to be interpreted as weakness. In 1959 another destructive intruder arrived at Chinatown's doorstep, this time from City Hall itself.

An ordinance approved by the Chicago City Council in 1959 authorized the Chicago Housing Authority to acquire property in Chinatown between 23rd Place and 24th Street and from Stewart to Princeton Avenues to expand the Archer Courts public housing project. Although crowded conditions and the shortage of housing in Chinatown had reached critical proportions, local residents did not see public housing as a solution. Despite low incomes, most Chinese had accumulated some savings and therefore would be ineligible for public housing. Furthermore, they resisted dependence upon the government and preferred to find housing on their own. Finally, residents and merchants alike feared that the new public housing project would change the character of their neighborhood.

The Challenge

It was at this time that Chinatown's local leadership began to play a pivotal role. Several businessmen realized that middle-income Chinese would have to remain, while others would have to be attracted back, in order to reverse the area's decline. With the growth of a middle class would come home ownership, improvement of housing, greater patronage of local businesses and more forceful civic involvement on behalf of better schools, parks and city services.

Good housing at exceptionally attractive prices was identified as the key to holding the Chinese middle class. New issues had to be addressed: How could housing be developed when there was little privately owned land remaining? Would for-profit developers drive new housing prices unattractively high? Would lenders be willing to make long-term loans?

A small group of Chinese-American businessmen decided to inject new energy into their community by providing attractive housing at below-market prices through a not-for-profit development corporation. The emergence of these community leaders to resist City Hall's plans was significant. They set on a course of aggressive self-help that was dramatic, especially when viewed in the light of their community's earlier submissiveness to external threats.

The businessmen's initiative crystallized the Chinese community's realization that acquiescence to City Hall's plan for their neighborhood would defeat them totally. They had to take control of their community or lose it. The current president of the Chinatown Chamber of Commerce, Ping Tom, summed up the opinion prevailing two decades earlier:

> For so long we tried to keep the outside away from our community. Every time the city or state authorities came in, we did not say a thing. That is why we lost so much land. We lost housing for 562 families because the State said, "Maybe a highway will come through here."

> We can no longer afford being the subservient, reserved, shy people. We have got to participate in the 20th century.[2]

Three business and civic leaders took the initiative in 1959. Harry Tom was the owner of China Maid products, China Garden Restaurant and Min Sun Trading Company. William Wong Way owned the Lekel Chop Suey Pail Company. And Gung-Hsing Wang (better known as G.H. Wang), was an insurance broker and a former Chinese consul in Chicago. In the 1950s Wang had served as executive director of the Chinese American Civic Council, the local community organization. The trio was able to convince John D'Arco, their alderman, and the City Council, that a public housing project would not be necessary because the Chinese community itself would build housing to meet the needs of its residents.

Within two months Tom, Way and Wang had formed the not-for-profit Chinatown Redevelopment Association (CRA), and their renewal effort was underway. Tom became its president, William Way the vice-president, and Wang the managing director. The situation in Chinatown at the time that they organized CRA was described as follows:

> When Wang began, housing was deteriorating. According to one newspaper account at the time, more than half the residential units were classified as substandard. People were moving away, and the community seemed to face a sure, if slow, death.[3]

The Neighborhood Strategy

The Chinatown Redevelopment Association (CRA) initially had three objectives: (a) to rehabilitate and restore the neighborhood generally known as Chinatown; (b) to build and sell residential properties to meet the housing needs of Chinese-Americans on a not-for-profit basis; and (c) to build, own and operate residential properties on a cooperative basis.[4] These objectives were grounded in the philosophy expressed by Wang:

> Stability is in the heart. The people who live here have to take pride and feed their roots. One good way to accomplish this is to get them to invest. Once you own property you want the community to thrive, the schools to improve.[5]

The CRA approach would give the Chinese-American middle class a stake in the neighborhood by making good housing available at affordable prices. For the residents to identify closely with the community, any new housing would have to be owned and not just rented. It was important to give people a piece of land and a sense of ownership in the community. As Wang was ready to point out:

> In the case of Chinatown, the first approach to the revitalization of a depressed neighborhood is the retention of moderate-income families. Once neighborhood self-confidence is established, then you can get into low-income housing. When low-income development precedes moderate-income development, it leads to the departure of the moderate-income families.[6]

The first focus, therefore, of the Chinatown Redevelopment Association would be residential development for moderate-income households. Good homes had to be built and offered at attractive prices to retain or lure back the middle-income families that would become the backbone of the community. When such families acquired a financial and personal stake in Chinatown, their community would stabilize and grow. The middle class would provide the consumer base necessary to help support local retailers and other businesses.

Ultimately, the CRA's goal was to revive the self-confidence of residents and to change the outside world's image of the neighborhood. Once these goals were accomplished, the private sector and the real estate market would take over and generate their own momentum. The need for the not-for-profit housing developer would then end. To Wang, the interventionist role of the CRA was clear. Its purpose was not to provide housing to all those in need, nor to meet the entire demand for new housing, but rather to stimulate the housing market so that for-profit developers would find it worthwhile to take over.[7]

Hurdling Obstacles

The situation in Chicago's Chinatown was even worse than it appeared to the fledgling developers. According to an account in a national newspaper, Chinatown was:

> an area of much substandard housing where it was impossible to get an FHA loan, where banks were not interested in lending, and where the city was ready to move in with a housing project....[8]

Years later, Wang recalled that:

> a former director of the Federal Housing Administration, in response to an application for mortgage insurance in Chinatown,

had written: "influences exist in the neighborhood which preclude eligibility and most certainly would limit economic life and mortgage term."

To those who wanted to improve the neighborhood, this blunt opinion from a high-ranking federal official woke them up from an "ask the government to do it" dream. The choice became "sink or swim," and we decided to swim.[9]

Four major hurdles challenged the ingenuity and leadership of the Chinatown Redevelopment Association:

• The lack of working capital. The CRA had few resources with which to begin. How could a development organization be run without capital? What would be the source for operating and investment capital?

• The reluctance of major lenders to make loans. These were the days before "red-lining" became a public issue, when lenders could seal the fate of a community by their own perceptions of its future.

• The need to make housing not only competitive in terms of quality, but also at a lesser price than could be found elsewhere. In order for the upwardly mobile Chinese to be persuaded to stay in this sad, little neighborhood and for the successful people who had already left to come back, they had to be offered an exceptionally good buy. The challenge to the CRA was, then, to construct better-than-average housing at an affordable price. Part of the solution was already at hand. The cost of the new housing would be reduced because the CRA would forego a profit.

• The unavailability of privately owned and vacant land of adequate size for housing development. High visibility and "critical mass" were important to ensure the success of the project.

To purchase the land and launch the development, Harry Tom and William Way, officers of the CRA, each signed a personal note as collateral for a $30,000 loan from the Central National Bank to purchase land and launch the development. The reluctance of lenders to make construction or permanent mortgage loans in the area was an even tougher barrier to overcome, but the CRA's persistence was eventually rewarded. As Wang remembered it:

I spent one month knocking on the doors of lending agencies and banks. No results. Then one day I was telling my experience to an acquaintance in a savings and loan association, and I remarked, half jokingly, "I know your institution wouldn't lend us anything." "Why are you so sure?" he wanted to know. His company, the Chicago Federal Savings and Loan Association, issued a blanket mortgage of $104,000 for construction of eight town houses on vacant property, and our building program began.[10]

The first two loans of $30,000 for working capital, however, were not enough. The ultimate solution alleviated other problems as well. The town houses that the CRA planned to build would be pre-sold before construction began. Large down payments would be required, about thirty percent of the purchase price. The large down payments would be used as capital to finance the construction, thus reducing the amount of initial debt and helping leverage interim financing from lenders. While the incomes of most Chinese households were quite low, they were a thrifty people and hence managed to accumulate savings. Putting aside money so that they could own property was almost an obsession with them.

The shortage of vacant and privately owned land available for development in Chinatown was circumvented by the resourceful utilization of undeveloped public land. In the first phase of development under the CRA, the land acquired included vacant sites privately owned but previously designated for public housing. On occasion the CRA also resorted to the acquisition of privately owned land with dilapidated structures requiring demolition. (In the second phase under the Neighborhood Redevelopment Assistance Inc., surplus expressway land owned by the State of Illinois was acquired.) The purchase of public lands had two advantages, low cost and absence of existing structures. All the pieces came together for the first phase of town house construction in 1960.

The Town Houses

Between 1960 and 1964, the Chinatown Redevelopment Association constructed a total of twenty-eight town houses. The first ten were adjoining town houses along the 300 block of West 24th Street between Princeton and Stewart Avenues. The site was the one previously designated by the City for the construction of a public housing project. Instead, the City was persuaded to allow the CRA to purchase and develop the site for much needed private housing.

These town houses followed the Chinese custom whereby houses were located close together for mutual protection. With this tradition in mind, the CRA designed a row of eight, and another of two, connected units. Each town house contained a spacious combination living room/dining room and kitchen on the first floor, three bedrooms and a bath on the second floor, together with a full basement. An oriental design on the brick exterior was replicated on the wrought iron fence which encircled the homes and their adjoining yards. The idea of an oriental-style, tile roof was discarded because of its high cost.

The CRA was able to offer its first set of town houses at prices between $19,000 and $20,000, well below the purchase price of comparable buildings in nearby neighborhoods. All ten buyers were Chinese, three of whom had moved out of the neighborhood and wanted to come back when the opportunity presented itself. The CRA strategy had begun to take hold.

In 1961 the CRA came out with a second complex of town houses, also uniquely designed. This time the eight-unit development was structured in a U-shape, with a sunken garden courtyard reminiscent of village compounds in China. (The sunken garden had its practical aspects because Chinatown's sidewalks were vaulted. The lot level was almost three feet lower than the street. To bring the lot level up to the street would require a costly landfill and the building of retaining walls. The U-shaped design of the garden used the building itself for retaining walls.) The units with three bedrooms and one and one-half baths sold for $23,000, and the four bedroom units with two full baths sold for $24,000. This development was located at the northeast corner of 23rd Street and Princeton Avenue.

By 1964 ten more town houses were developed by the CRA along the 2300 block of South Princeton Avenue and the 300 block of West 23rd Street. Between 1960 and 1964 the CRA had brought new life to Chinatown with the presence of twenty-eight new town houses.

The fact that all twenty-eight town houses were readily sold prior to construction spoke well of the credibility of the developers. All of the home buyers were Chinese-Americans. The only negative reaction came when the demand exceeded the supply. Disappointed, would-be buyers did not understand that the CRA's resources were limited. In some cases prospective buyers

The Town Houses of Chinatown: Phase I

Developer: Chinatown Redevelopment Association

Units: Twenty-eight town houses for sale

            Three bedrooms and 1 1/2 baths or four bed-
            rooms with two baths

            All with full basements

Location: Chinatown

            308-326 W. 24th Street (ten town houses)

            260-266 W. 23rd Place and 2315-2321 S.
            Princeton (eight town houses)

            2301-2307 S. Princeton (four town houses)

            341-351 W. 23rd Place (six town houses)

Years of Completion: 1961-1965

Initial Prices: $19,000-$24,000

Financing: Land acquisition loan: Central National Bank

            Construction loan: thirty percent down pay-
            ment by buyers, remainder from Chicago
            Federal Savings and Loan

            Permanent mortgages: Chicago Federal Sav-
            ings and Loan

Architect: Robert Saichek

Contractors: Dahl Construction Company, primarily

mistakenly believed that a private, not-for-profit developer had an obligation to accommodate everyone.

Neighborhood Renewal

The twenty-eight town houses built by the Chinatown Redevelopment Association helped generate, among residents, the commitment needed for Chinatown's renewal. During the pivotal 1960s, when investors were found for the first round of town houses, other key institutions began to invest in Chinatown. A $500,000 addition to the Chinese Christian Union Church on the 2300 block of Wentworth was initiated and subsequently completed; a new annex, called the "bachelor quarters," was added to Chinatown's apartment house for returning servicemen; and St. Therese Mission School constructed an entirely new school building costing $380,000. On their own, some residents either built or renovated their own homes. Today, Chinatown's side streets are lined with well-maintained older buildings, interspersed with new homes.

By April 1964, approximately five years after CRA's leaders had taken their initiative, over $2.5 million had been invested by local residents and businesses in residential, commercial, industrial and institutional developments. No public money was utilized.[11]   Chinatown had begun to rejuvenate itself and was attracting new investors from both inside and outside the community. Major newspapers wrote feature stories about Chinatown. *The Christian Science Monitor*, for example, hailed "Chicago's Chinatown: From Darkness Into Light." The tourist trade, an important source of income for Chinatown's economy, increased considerably, thereby stimulating restaurants and shops to invest further in expansion and facade improvements.

By 1966 Chinatown's leaders had achieved much of what they had set out to do seven years earlier. The middle class was once again able to make Chinatown its home. The private market had been stimulated. Businesses were beginning to prosper, Chinese cultural and social institutions were strengthened, and Chinatown was no longer a feeble neighborhood that could be nibbled away by outside interests. It was finally on the map. The CRA's hopes for Chinatown had come to pass. The Chinatown Redevelopment Association, a not-for-profit organization, had become an amazing enterprise. Without realizing it, the CRA discovered that it had made a "profit," while many other for-profit housing developers, even those insured by the federal

The Town Houses of Chinatown

government, were showing a loss. The CRA turned its surplus over to the Internal Revenue Service. With no working capital, the leaders of the CRA decided it was time to close their doors. Harry Tom and William Way simply carried on with their respective businesses. Wang became the assistant director and subsequently the administrator of the City of Chicago's own housing corporation: the Chicago Dwellings Association. Then he became the housing director for the Chicago Model Cities Program.

Neighborhood Redevelopment Assistance

While working for the City of Chicago's Model Cities Program, Wang continued to follow Chinatown's revitalization efforts. He began to realize that despite the housing initiatives that had already been undertaken, there was still a shortage of affordable housing units. There was still work to be done in developing housing in Chinatown. In 1972, in anticipation of his retirement from government service, Wang obtained the permission of Model Cities Director Erwin A. France to organize a not-for-profit community improvement organization, the Neighborhood Redevelopment Assistance Inc. (NRA), with a 501(c)3 status. In 1976 Wang left Model Cities in order to devote full time to the NRA.

The pieces of Wang's new development vehicle were already in place and in operation. Thomas A. Volini, a former associate from the Model Cities Program, who shared Wang's social commitment, was engaged as the NRA's attorney. James Swann was recruited for architectural services. A variety of contractors would be utilized. Two lending institutions became the financial backers: Lakeside Bank and First Federal Savings and Loan Association.

By this time Chinatown's future was assured. The middle class was visibly present. The commercial area along Wentworth had become a major tourist attraction featuring two dozen restaurants and fourteen gift shops. Chinatown also supported three bakeries, an herb store, three noodle factories, two barber shops, two travel agencies, an Oriental folk music club and a martial arts school. The St. Therese Mission School and Chinese Christian Union Church continued to thrive.

Chinatown's population in 1974 had grown to approximately 5,000, eighty percent of whom were Chinese, the rest being primarily black or Italian.[12] The addition of the twenty-eight town houses which the CRA had built, plus the housing units newly built or renovated by Chinatown's own merchants and property owners, did not eliminate the shortage of good housing. Average household income was still low, especially among the neighborhood's 1,000 elderly.[13]

Because the demand for housing still exceeded the supply, property values had skyrocketed. Older three-flats selling for $25,000 in 1959 were selling for $55-65,000 by 1974. [14] The increase in property values within a renewed Chinatown had actually created wealth for its residents and investors. Immigrant families were still coming into the neighborhood at the rate of about fifteen to twenty per month. Characteristically, crime and dependence on public welfare continued to be nearly nonexistent.

Within this community environment, the NRA set about its task of providing additional housing of good quality at affordable prices and contributing further to the revitalization of Chinatown. By the end of 1979 the NRA had, with its development team, completed the construction of thirty-eight new town houses, a twelve-unit condominium, and a 139-unit apartment building for the elderly, the Tsee-Ying Apartments. (Note: the elderly apartments are the subject of the next chapter.)

Wang continued to use the formula that had worked so well with the Chinatown Redevelopment Association: building on bargain-priced, surplus government land wherever possible, pre-selling the units to use the equity of large down payments to reduce the costs of construction financing, and using a private, not-for-profit vehicle.

There were some differences, however, between the approach of the CRA in Phase I and that of the NRA in Phase II. One factor was the availability of financing in Phase II. With a respectable track record behind him, Wang had little trouble obtaining the working capital he needed or permanent financing for the NRA town houses and condominiums. Another variance was the exclusive use of surplus government land in Phase II, primarily excess expressway property. It was not necessary, therefore, to resort to the acquisition of privately owned sites with existing structures as was sometimes the case in the first round of development under the CRA.

A third difference in Phase II was NRA's emphasis on detached houses rather than on the row houses characteristic of the

The Town Houses of Chinatown: Phase II

Developer: Neighborhood Redevelopment Assistance Inc.

Units: Thirty-eight town houses for sale
           Twelve condominium units for sale

Location: Chinatown
           220-256 W. 25th Place (fourteen town hous-
           es)
           2536-2558 S. Wentworth (twelve town hous-
           es)
           203-239 W. 24th Place (twelve town houses)
           2417-2425 S. Wentworth (twelve condomin-
           iums)

Years of Completion: 1974-1979

Initial Prices: $27,500-$37,000

Financing: Construction loans: thirty percent down pay-
           ment by buyers, remainder from the Lakeside
           Bank
           Permanent mortgages: First Federal Savings
           and Loan Association

Architect: Swann & Weiskopf

Contractors: Various companies

CRA's Phase I construction. According to Wang, the shift to detached houses was intended to reduce the potential for disagreement among owners over common walls. The fourth difference in Phase II was the experiment with condominium development. The final difference was the way that the NRA used its surplus. This time around, excess revenues were put back into the town houses for such improvements as additional landscaping and fencing. Thus the new owners received more than they had been promised.

The NRA town houses along 25th Place sold for $29,000, along 24th Place for $30,000 and along Wentworth for $37,000. The three-bedroom, two-bath condominiums on Wentworth sold for $27,500. The sales price on these buildings was again much lower than the cost of comparable buildings in adjoining neighborhoods. The NRA set certain requirements for those to whom it was willing to sell. The potential buyers had to be current or former residents of Chinatown, had to qualify for a mortgage, and had to permit the use of their early down payment for construction financing.

Buyers who were civic leaders and local business people were given preference because their continued presence would also have a catalytic effect upon the community. That is why the NRA allotted some of its units to buyers referred by the alderman of the First Ward. (The NRA learned that in Chicago political good will was essential to community improvement.) Generally, these buyers were of Italian background and settled themselves in the town houses along 25th Place, while those of Chinese origin were attracted to the town houses along 24th Place. Of the sixty-eight town houses built by the CRA and the NRA, ten were purchased by Italian-Americans.

In acquiring the 2.2 acres of surplus expressway land at the appraised, fair-market value of $125,000, the NRA encountered an unusual problem and solved it with an equally unusual approach. The surplus land consisted of four irregularly shaped parcels, two along the Stevenson Expressway and two along the Dan Ryan Expressway. Because of the zoning, only one building was allowed on each of the four lots, unless the lots were subdivided. Since the four sites were irregular, they could neither be subdivided nor provide front and rear setbacks. The NRA overcame the obstacle by obtaining the City's approval to develop the four sites as a single PUD (Planned Unit Development), thereby enabling the NRA to construct thirty-eight town houses and a twelve-unit condominium, all in conformity with the building and zoning codes. Lakeside Bank provided the temporary construction financing, while First Federal Savings and Loan granted the permanent mortgages. As with the town houses, the buyers of the condominium units were required to make large down payments of thirty percent or more, in advance.

The NRA chose to use condominiums rather than cooperatives because of its sensitivity to the Chinese-American preference for individual ownership. According to Wang, another Chinese cultural trait, that of decision-making by consensus, made management of the twelve-unit condominium difficult and discouraged the NRA from further attempts at condominium development.

By 1979 when Wang had completed the Tsee-Ying Apartments and had retired from an active role in housing development, Chinatown was basking in the glow of renewal. Its population had risen to more than 8,000 by 1984, with immigrants still arriving at the rate of about 500 each year. New construction of both residential and commercial properties and remodeling of existing structures continued. Some property values within the neighborhood were estimated to have increased tenfold since 1959 . Private developers were still making a profit with their new construction. Seeking to capitalize on the area's turnabout, the suburban Elmhurst Federal Savings and Loan Association opened a Chicago-based branch in Chinatown in December 1975.

Carl M. Grip, executive director of the South Side Planning Board, identified an unexpected benefit from Chinatown's resurgence:

> The work of G.H. Wang and his associates went beyond Chinatown. Its revitalization helped hold together the home owners who peopled the predominantly Italian-American neighborhood immediately to the south.[15]

In 1987 Chinatown was, in fact, bursting at the seams and searching for more land on which to expand. A rare sight in Chinatown is a vacant lot. Along the neighborhood's side streets, almost every square foot of land contains a building. As a result, civic leaders set their sights on developing thirty-seven acres north of Cermak Road acquired by the Chinese American Development Corporation from the Santa Fe Railway. That land is to be developed for residential and retail use. By moving northward, Chinatown was heading toward the original Chinese settlement a century earlier at the edge of Chicago's central business district. In addition, Chinatown had begun to expand westward as its commercial and residential development skipped over the Santa Fe railway tracks to Canal Street.

The resilience of Chinese communities across the United States was documented in a report, "Chinatowns Stand Their Ground," in *Planning,* published by the American Planning Association. Appraising the state of Chinatowns in Houston, Boston, New York, Oakland and San Francisco, that study came to a conclusion that applied as well to their counterpart in Chicago:

> Today, Chinese-American enclaves all over the U.S. continue to thrive--in much the same location and manner as they did a century ago. Considering the tendency of immigrants to disperse and the transformation that U.S. cities have experienced, the staying power of the Chinese settlements is remarkable.[16]

Reflections of the Developer

G.H. Wang reminisced in 1986 about his experiences with the town house developments, reflecting both his sense of accomplishment and his rueful feeling that his purposes were not always understood by the community he served:

> We were successful in proving the point that a private, not-for-profit developer of affordable housing can generate an attractive housing market to benefit for-profit developers. The shortcoming was that the public did not understand that a private, not-for-profit developer could not be expected to build homes for everybody at affordable prices. The principal goal of a not-for-profit developer is to carry out a public purpose and not to meet the private demand for housing.[17]

> We planted a seed to generate neighborhood confidence in the viability of Chinatown. I think it has taken roots.[18]

When asked about what he would have done differently, Wang's penchant for the long-term perspective showed itself. He would have liked to make wider use of pre-stressed, concrete modular construction that is wear-and-tear proof. He hoped that someday Chicago's building codes and union rules will easily permit the use of materials and systems that are more lasting, efficient and affordable than housing built on-site, with traditional materials and construction methods.

The development of Chinatown's town houses also demonstrated the viability of a neighborhood renewal strategy. The usual guideline for community revitalization is a tri-partite model: a development mechanism which involves the local community, the private developer and the public sector. In the case of Chinatown the principal role was played by the community itself, with the public and private sectors playing supporting roles. It is the story of a people who, discriminated against in the past but drawing strength from their culture, shaped their own future and the destiny of their neighborhood.

The successful construction of housing by a pioneering, not-for-profit corporation can encourage further housing construction by others, including for-profit developers. The Cacciatore Company, which built the NRA's town houses on 25th Place and Wentworth Avenue and on 26th Street, went on to develop its own housing south of 25th Place. Its subsequent success confirmed that Chinatown was ready for the appearance of for-profit developers and that local residents would buy homes on the fringes of Chinatown, thereby marking the beginning of Chinatown's expansion.

NOTES

1.   Beginning in 1882, a series of "Chinese Exclusion Acts" suspended Chinese immigration to the United States. In 1924, the United States opened its doors to a mere 105 Chinese immigrants a year. In 1943 the Chinese Exclusion Acts were repealed and for the first time Chinese were granted the right to naturalized citizenship and the right to own real estate. By 1952, in response to the Communist takeover of mainland China, Congress passed the Refugee Relief Act which allowed Chinese refugees to enter the United States. Many came to Chicago. In the 1960s immigration laws were further liberalized to allow the reuniting of families. This brought even more people to Chicago's Chinatown.

2.   Howard Witt, "Chinatown confronting a great wall--hemmed in on three sides--community looks for way to grow," *Chicago Tribune* (April 8, 1984), Section 4, p.1.

3. Delia O'Hara, "Developer Wang builds Chinatown's fortune," *Chicago Sun-Times* (February 15, 1980), p.80. A description of the renewal of Chicago's Chinatown with a focus on Gung-Hsing Wang and the role he played.

4. As quoted in "Chinatown Builds for the Future," *The Guarantor* (October 1960). A description of the early stage of Chinatown's renewal.

5. Delia O'Hara, p.81.

6. Gung-Hsing Wang, interview January 6, 1986.

7. Gung-Hsing Wang.

8. Dorothea Kahn Jaffe, "Chicago's Chinatown: From Darkness Into Light. Do-it-yourself Renewal Pays Off," *The Christian Science Monitor* (July 17,1962), p.C3. A tribute to the dramatic reversal of Chinatown's condition and the self-help process that brought it about.

9. *Bulletin* of the Chicago Metropolitan Chapter of the National Association of Housing and Redevelopment Officials (March 1977), p.3.

10. Dorothea Kahn Jaffe, p.C3.

11. Sheila Wolfe, "Chinatown District Undergoes Operation to Lift Its Face--Non-profit Group Spearheads Renewal," *Chicago Tribune* (April 12, 1964).

12. Don DeBat, "Chinatown: Quiet Island," *Chicago Daily News* (July 5,1974), p.8. A profile of Chicago's Chinatown, with interviews of prominent leaders.

13. Letter from Gung-Hsing Wang to P.S. Caplan, Economic and Market Analysis Division of the U.S. Department of Housing and Urban Development, December 5, 1977.

14. Don DeBat, p.8.

15. Carl M. Grip, interview December 30, 1987.

16. Todd W. Bressi, "Chinatowns Stand Their Ground," *Planning* (November 1987), p.13.

17. Gung-Hsing Wang.

18. Gung-Hsing Wang, interview August 10, 1986.

3

The Tsee-Ying
Apartments

The demand for housing for the elderly is still great. In America, as affluent as we are, the need for standard housing at an affordable price is desperate. Somehow we have not found a practical way of meeting the need.-- Gung-Hsing Wang

Three social considerations guided the development of a unique, nine-story, 139-unit apartment complex for low-income elderly located in Chicago's Chinatown neighborhood. The developer, Neighborhood Redevelopment Assistance Inc., sought (a) to supply good housing for Chinatown's low-income elderly; (b) to demonstrate how such housing could be made more affordable by using prefabricated, interlocking, concrete panel construction; and (c) to build on land formerly owned by the Chicago Housing Authority in order to show that public and private housing agencies can cooperate.

Remembering the Elderly

The Tsee-Ying Elderly Apartments, a striking nine-story building, is situated one block west of Wentworth Avenue, Chinatown's main street. The high rise is an imposing structure not only for its size but also for its design: a sloped tile roof in the oriental style, and a panel on the facade with a motif of Chinese characters which spell out "Chicago's mansion for honored

The Tsee-Ying Apartments

elderly." A generous, landscaped park is in the rear. The building, which was completed in 1979, contains 139 one-bedroom apartments, each with approximately 630 square feet of living space. The modest rent levels, construction of high quality, and convenient location make it a desirable residence for elderly wishing to remain close to their relatives and to centers of Chinese culture. (In 1987 the waiting list counted 150 households, the demand far exceeding the supply.)

In addition to providing badly needed housing and demonstrating the use of cost-reducing construction methods, the Tsee-Ying Apartments, also known as the Chinatown Elderly Apartments, spurred further the revitalization of once-depressed Chinatown.

The Setting in the 1970s

In 1987 Chicago's Chinatown enjoyed a fair measure of renewal, prosperity and confidence in its future. This was not the situation twenty-five years earlier. In the early 1960s the area between Archer Avenue and 25th Street, Stewart Avenue and the New York Central Railroad tracks near LaSalle Street was in deteriorating condition. The majority of residents were Chinese, many of them recent immigrants of limited means. A significant percentage of the housing was owned by an earlier ethnic group, the Italians, many of whom had begun moving to other areas. Furthermore, in 1959 the City of Chicago had decided to build more public housing in Chinatown. Its leaders then realized that they themselves must take prime responsibility for plotting their community's future.

Under their leadership Chinatown's middle-income residents had, by the early 1970s, begun to enjoy their new town houses and to benefit from rising property values. Local businesses shared in the growing prosperity. A Chicago neighborhood, once on the verge of collapse, had renewed itself while enriching the city's ethnic diversity. (See the previous case study, "The Town Houses of Chinatown.")

For one group, however, revitalization of Chinatown was a mixed blessing. For the indigent elderly, the neighborhood's new prosperity meant that competition for the scarce supply of housing would be keener. Even with the addition of new housing units built by non-profit and for-profit developers, there was still a net loss of 188 units between 1960 and 1970. The neigh-

The Tsee-Ying Apartments

Developers: Neighborhood Redevelopment Assistance Inc. and The Lombard Company

Units: 139 one-bedroom rental units

Location: Chicago's Chinatown
            Northwest corner of 23rd Street and Princeton Avenue on a 40,000 square foot site

Year of Completion: 1979

Cost of Project: $4,616,148

Initial Rent: $418 per month

Financing: Construction loan: Percy Wilson Mortgage Company

Permanent mortgage: $4,000,000 from Percy Wilson Mortgage Company, with FHA, 221(d)4 insurance and a forty-year term at affixed rate of 7.5%

Rent reductions through Section 8 housing assistance payments

Architect: Duane E. Linden and Associates

Contractor: The Lombard Company

borhood's total housing stock had dropped from 1,534 units in 1960 to 1,346 in 1970, principally as a result of the construction of the expressways at its edges.[1]

By 1970, middle-income Chinese families were paying rents of $125 to $250 a month. Many of the elderly, however, could afford monthly rents of no more than $60 to $100. Of the 4,730 Chinese counted in the neighborhood, approximately 950 were elderly, their average annual income less than $2,000.[2] (At that time the U.S. Department of Housing and Urban Development's definition of "very poor tenancy" was an income of less than $6,969 for a one-person household and $7,969 for two.)

While working for the Chicago Model Cities Program in the 1970s, G.H. Wang had established the private, not-for-profit Neighborhood Redevelopment Assistance (NRA) with other Chinese businessmen.[3] Initially his intent was to construct additional town houses to expand housing opportunities for middle-income households in Chinatown.

However, as his projected retirement in 1976 from the Model Cities Program approached, Wang broadened his goals for the NRA. He recalled:

> No organized attempt had been made to house the elderly. Little rental housing was available in Chinatown. Somebody would have to do it, and Neighborhood Redevelopment Assistance was the only not-for-profit supplier of housing in Chinatown.[4]

The NRA accepted responsibility to develop decent housing for Chinatown's low-income elderly. Constructing apartments for the elderly was straightforward enough, but the challenge was to make them more affordable for the indigent.

Wang had seen the merits of factory-built, pre-cast, interlocking concrete panels used in a small residential property on 3726 West Flournoy Street in Chicago, built in the late 1960s by Michael Lombard of The Lombard Company. (The Flournoy building is now a pre-school center operated by the not-for-profit HICA Corporation of North Lawndale.) Wang decided to use Lombard's construction experience for the Tsee-Ying Apartments. Wang knew that pre-cast concrete used on Flournoy Street had demonstrated longer economic life and had retained its durability despite intensive, heavy usage by small children. The Lombard Company also had the rights to an innovative European process for the construction of multi-story buildings: the use of prefabricated and pre-stressed concrete panels each about seventy-five square feet in size, and weighing about three tons. The panel construction was "weather proof"; it could be manufactured by union labor in a factory, regardless of weather conditions. The 6,000-pound panels were used for framing the exterior facade and, because of their unusual strength, for structural supporting columns and weight-bearing walls. This system also involved the prefabrication of concrete floor sections with a hollow core. These sections could then be fitted together on site by a crane at a pace of about one floor per week.

This approach would cut interest costs by shortening the time period of the construction loan, because pre-cast panels, functioning as structural supports and the "skin" of the building, would be installed in a matter of weeks. Conventional, on-site construction would have taken much longer. The lesser maintenance costs of the concrete construction would be another cost-saving advantage, as the Flournoy building had demonstrated.

Another noteworthy technique, not originally anticipated by the developer, provided a solution to a larger organizational and financial problem. HUD required that the NRA trim $600,000 of the development costs, which exceeded HUD's maximum for an insurable loan. Wang was then confronted with the choice of either compromising the quality of his construction or finding an enterprising answer to HUD's demand without sacrificing quality. Since demonstrating the lasting quality of concrete construction was one of Wang's basic objectives, another solution had to be found. The unique answer came in finding a for-profit partner who could use losses as a tax advantage. The Lombard Company was willing to reduce its construction charges in return for an interest as a limited partner with Neighborhood Redevelopment Assistance Corporation.This step was a singular achievement: a for-profit contractor was helping a not-for-profit housing sponsor realize its original goals. (Alone as a not-for-profit sponsor of housing, the NRA would not have been able to build the Tsee-Ying Apartments for the elderly; it was rescued by a new and for-profit co-sponsor.)

With the help of its enterprising attorney, the NRA persuaded the FHA to insure a mortgage on a property not owned by the

NRA but only leased to it for seventy-five years. To make such an unusual arrangement legal, approval had to be obtained from no less than seven entities: the Percy Wilson Mortgage Company, the Federal National Mortgage Association ("Fannie Mae"), the U.S. Department of Housing and Urban Development, the Office of the Governor of Illinois, the Illinois State Housing Board, the Illinois Department of Revenue and the Chicago Housing Authority.

Serving Neighborhood Residents

How would rents be made more affordable? This would be done, of course, through HUD's Section 8 Housing Assistance Payment program. Under this program eligible tenants are required to pay no more than twenty-five percent (later revised upward to thirty percent) of their income for rent and utilities, with the remainder to be paid by HUD. The use of Section 8 subsidies is a commonly employed tool, even for lower-income families in some luxury-type apartment complexes near Chicago's downtown area.

Developers of government-subsidized housing, even for the elderly, often encounter varying degrees of community resistance. The hostility is based upon the residents' real or imagined fears that the new housing would lower real estate values. This opposition did not occur, however, in the case of the Tsee-Ying Apartments. Wang received community support because of the special esteem and sense of responsibility that Chinese people have for their elderly. Further, the community was confident that many of its elderly would occupy the building. Wang recalled:

> You do not present a concept or an idea to the public until you
> have a detailed project: land, financing, architecture. Otherwise
> you just have talk, talk, talk, and you get nowhere.[5]

Usually, developers present their own plan first and then allow constituents to react to it, rather than ask them to develop a plan of their own from ground zero. Confident of his perception of what his people's needs were and what could be done about them, Wang proceeded to follow his own intuition and experience. By early 1978 when he announced publicly the NRA's development plan for the elderly apartments, he had already put the pieces together. This approach, according to Wang, is fair to the community. It is not an idea or a plan subject to "ifs" and "whens" but a definite development with all particulars in place and with sufficient flexibility to meet any needs that may have been neglected. At this point, the development was less than one year from completion.

The Actual Development Process

The choice of contractor was easy because it had been Michael Lombard who had demonstrated to Wang the efficacy of prefabricated, interlocking, concrete panels and who had an interest in proving their utility. Duane E. Linden Associates were selected as the architects because of their knowledge of panel construction and their sensitivity to the oriental motif that was to become the development's visual hallmark. Wang's former associate at Model Cities, Thomas A. Volini, was retained as the NRA's general counsel. Volini had also left the Chicago Model Cities Program to establish a private law practice with a special interest in law governing real estate ventures.

Earlier, in the summer of 1975, Wang had arranged for a commitment by the Chicago Housing Authority (CHA) to lease a 40,000 square foot site at 23rd Street and Princeton Avenue for seventy-five years at the price of $14,400 per year. The agreement provided that the CHA itself would obtain the zoning changes needed to construct the elderly apartments. In June 1976, HUD's Chicago Area Director, John L. Waner, approved Wang's application for insurance and the all-essential Housing Assistance Payments contract which would subsidize rents with The Lombard Company and Michael Lombard as limited partners.

In November 1976, Wang applied for FHA mortgage insurance under HUD's 221(d)(4) permanent financing program in the amount of $3,830,000. The construction loan was to be funded by Percy Wilson Mortgage Corporation. At that time the total estimated cost of the development was projected at $4,255,900. The partners' required equity was projected at $425,600.[6]

In April 1978, commitments were obtained from the FHA and Percy Wilson Mortgage Corporation as proposed. The Government National Mortgage Corporation committed itself to purchase the mortgage at the below-market interest rate of 7.5 percent. In the same month, the building's foundation was laid. During the previous winter the concrete panels had been manufactured to specifications in a factory located in the Chicago area. As the weather became warmer, the panels were put into place. Potential conflict with labor unions over the use of prefabricated construction was avoided by employing union labor in the factory where the panels were formed, as well as in the installation on site and for the interior work.

In November 1978, the recruitment of tenants began. A marketing survey initiated prior to the beginning of construction indicated that the local demand for the apartments was almost twice the number of units to be constructed. To assure a careful and impartial selection of tenants, the NRA employed the services of a Ph.D. candidate in social science at the University of Chicago. He visited each of the applicants in their old apartments, assessed their housekeeping skills, and evaluated their qualifications in accordance with the HUD-approved fair housing plan and the Section 8 selection guidelines. The Ph.D. candidate was later hired as the on-site building manager. And a professional management company was engaged to attend to fiscal, maintenance, reporting and other technical details. By April 1979, the first occupants of Tsee-Ying Apartments had moved in. By August 1979, all apartments were occupied, and the waiting list had sixty qualified applicants.

In July 1979, following completion of the development and when all the actual costs were known, the Neighborhood Redevelopment Assistance Corporation applied to the FHA through the Percy Wilson Mortgage Corporation, for an increase in the mortgage insurance from $3,830,000 to $4,000,000, which was granted. Ultimately, development costs amounted to $4,616,148. This final figure was $360,248 higher than the 1976 estimate.[7]

Despite the insurer's concern that the elderly tenants not be totally indigent, the developer clearly viewed the market as being those in desperate need. Under HUD guidelines eleven percent of the applicants qualified as "poor," while eighty-nine percent were "very poor."[8] The ethnic and racial composition mix of initial tenants was eighty-five percent Chinese and fifteen percent white and black. According to Wang, this reflected fairly the proportion of each racial group within the development's market area. By 1987 the proportion of Chinese tenants had risen to ninety percent.

Reflections of the Developer

In looking back on his experience, Wang admitted to being especially pleased with the Tsee-Ying Apartments, his largest single development. He had, to use his own words, built "a mansion for Chicago's revered elderly." He had successfully met a critical housing need for the elderly. His greatest challenge had been to keep the rent levels affordable, within HUD's guidelines and without a reduction in the quality of construction. To be sure, Tsee-Ying Apartments was an experiment, but one that he relished. Wang emphasized, "I am crazy about experiments because they lead to improvements."

Insistence on construction of high quality was crucial to Wang, for several reasons. The first was that he wanted his fellow Chinese-Americans to enjoy a building of which they could be proud and in which they would feel secure. Secondly, he wanted to demonstrate the utility of the pre-cast, concrete panel method, but was only willing to do so within the context of a superior building. Thirdly, he wanted to make a lasting contribution to the renewal of the Chinatown neighborhood and could only do so with a building that would be seen as a community improvement. His reasons were eminently practical. Wang was convinced that construction which resisted wear and tear would shave operating costs in the long run. This would also serve as a successful example so that more of such housing would be built for families of low and moderate incomes.

In Wang's words the "warm-hearted but cool-headed" approach to serving his community through housing was the prudent course to take and became an important ingredient in the success formula. He noted that developers must have a clear sense of the constraints under which they operate. On the one hand, they may promise tenants more and deliver less by overreaching their managerial skills. On the other hand, if they hastily contract for outside services, they may jeopardize the development's financial soundness by excessive maintenance and service costs. Finally, Wang placed his achievement in perspective, noting that professional and competent management, sensitive to the needs of tenants and the problems they face, is the final step in a viable development.

Wang wanted the Tsee-Ying Apartments to be a positive influence by virtue of good residents. "A poor person can be a more qualified tenant than a millionaire," Wang noted. He was elated when an enterprising developer built the 100-unit Oriental Terrace, a town house development across the street from his building for the elderly. Always sensitive to the impact of the government-owned public housing which had encroached upon the southwestern border of Chinatown, Wang said:

> It goes to show that a federally subsidized facility can be an asset to the community once the neighborhood has regained confidence in its own viability.[9]

NOTES

1. Letter from Gung-Hsing Wang to P.S. Caplan, Economic and Market Analysis Division of the U.S. Department of Housing and Urban Development, December 5, 1977.

2. Letter from Gung-Hsing Wang.

3. Gung-Hsing Wang memorandum to Erwin France, Administrative Assistant to the Mayor of Chicago, June 1, 1970. Wang studiously avoided any potential conflict of interest by clearing this enterprise with France, the director of the Chicago Model Cities Program. He also did not involve Neighborhood Redevelopment Assistance with any project sponsored by the Model Cities Program. Finally, he denied himself any significant financial benefit, in the form of a salary, in the NRA's development activities.

4. Gung-Hsing Wang, interview January 4, 1986.

5. Gung-Hsing Wang.

6. Neighborhood Redevelopment Assistance, Inc., Application for Project Mortgage Insurance, November 4, 1976.

7. NRA, Application for Mortgage Insurance Increase, July 3, 1979.

8. NRA, "Current Status of Prospective Residents," briefing to the Community Advisory Committee, January 17, 1979.

9. Gung-Hsing Wang, interview August 9, 1986.

4

Atrium Village

We began with no experience, little money and no clout.--William Leslie

The Setting

Harvey Zorbaugh described the cleavage between the very rich and the very poor on Chicago's Near North Side in 1929 in his classic urban study, *The Gold Coast and the Slum.*[1] In 1970, forty years later, not much had changed. The median income of Gold Coast residents was $58,000 while that of those living in the slum west of LaSalle Street was $2,800.[2]

The disparity was especially evident in the area around Division and Wells Streets. Empty lots were covered with broken glass while the "el" shrieked by, metal scraping metal. All of this, as well as the overflow of patrons from Wells Street's bars and porno shops, gathered no praise from local residents or guidebook writers. Upscale renters from nearby Sandburg Village seldom dared venture into the neighborhood, shadowed as it was by the high rises of Cabrini-Green Homes, the Chicago Housing Authority's giant public housing project. And the arty crowd from Old Town, several blocks to the north, never found a romantic garret in the neighborhood.

Most important, the upwardly mobile residents of Cabrini-Green, when they could afford to move out of public housing, lacked any local alternative in privately owned, affordable housing. The shortage of moderately priced housing for the upwardly mobile poor was also felt in the neighborhood itself. Local

51

churches and other community institutions increasingly found that once their leaders could afford to leave "the project," they had no choice but to leave the neighborhood as well. The loss of successful role models not only contributed to the instability of the area's institutions but to community life in general.

The Opportunity

Midway between the Gold Coast and the slum stood a large parcel of vacant and underused land, 90.3 acres in the area between Division Street and Chicago Avenue, LaSalle Drive and Orleans Street. In 1968 the Chicago Department of Urban Renewal (DUR) designated the area as "slum and blighted" and began planning for its redevelopment. Local churches, community groups and community residents provided input into a final plan. Extensive neighborhood discussion and public meetings resulted in the DUR report: *Redevelopment Plan for Slum and Blighted Area Redevelopment: Project Chicago-Orleans*.[3] The DUR plan's objectives, at the insistence of community groups, provided that the housing be available to all income levels and families with children. The wealthy Gold Coast and the public housing of Cabrini-Green would then be bridged by an area which supplied housing for both populations. The DUR plan also generally fit into Chicago's larger strategy for redevelopment of its central area. An earlier city-sponsored plan, *Chicago 21: A Plan for the Central Area Communities* (Chicago Department of Development and Planning, 1973), had listed Cabrini-Green as one of the plan's five "critical priorities." After the target area had been officially designated as slum and blighted, the DUR began buying the land and its deteriorating buildings.

Developer's Goals, Obstacles and Strategies

Traditional developers were skeptical of the DUR plan. Not only were they reluctant to venture into this "no man's land" to provide new housing exclusively for the middle class, but they were even more opposed to becoming partners in a housing complex that would be mixed racially and economically. In the late 1960s some developers of apartments like Sandburg Village, for higher-income and two-earner families, had ventured into a section of the area nearer the Gold Coast. But they were only willing to construct new housing for better-paid urban professionals.

In 1968 the leaders of five local churches who were among those active in shaping Project Chicago-Orleans formed the Chicago-Orleans Housing Corporation (COH).[4] The churches were: LaSalle Street, St. Matthew United Methodist, Holy

Family Lutheran, Fourth Presbyterian and St. Dominic. (St. Dominic Church was later forced to drop out of the COH by the late
Cardinal John Patrick Cody. Years later when Cardinal Joseph
Bernardin was appointed Archbishop of Chicago, St. Joseph
Catholic Church joined the consortium.) The COH board of directors was as diverse as the area it hoped to represent: a lawyer,
an architect, a day laborer, ministers, housewives and others.
Some 7,000 hours would eventually be volunteered by the COH
board members.

A Bridging Community

The COH was formed primarily to provide decent housing
for area residents with low and moderate incomes. In addition,
the COH hoped to build a bridging community, one that would
connect people of varying income levels and different races.
Furthermore, since it was the church leaders who had successfully insisted on the inclusion of housing for low-income families in
the DUR plan, it was incumbent on COH to make certain that this
objective was realized. One COH pastor explained his group's
perception of the situation:

> Gentrification has to come if there is to be revitalization. Dis-
> placement then follows. Why should upwardly mobile parishion-
> ers from Cabrini-Green be forced to move away? Why must peo-
> ple displaced by community improvements move out, decimating
> our leadership and volunteer network? Give them the opportunity
> to stay in the neighborhood, if that's their choice. If they want to
> keep their ties to our churches and schools, we need housing that
> will keep them around. We want, if we can, to hold that leader-
> ship in the neighborhood. Then we can stabilize our churches and
> provide models for other public housing residents.
>
> I know that the slums on the Lower North Side are legendary. But
> why should they continue for the next hundred years? I'm not an
> urban pessimist. We learn from the mistakes of the past. We will
> reclaim that land for decent housing and good neighboring.[5]

The goal of "good neighboring" added another dimension to
the development task that the COH had undertaken. The COH
churches not only wanted to provide decent housing for low-
income families, but they also wanted it done in such a way that
would make the middle class neighbors of the upwardly mobile
poor. This goal called for a housing development that would
reflect the larger area's economic and racial diversity.

Atrium Village

Housing for low-income households has often been designed like a series of boxes, in horizontal or vertical rows--like barracks facing in one direction. Neither the soldiers who lived in barracks nor the residents who occupied low-income housing were ever asked what they would prefer.

Since the COH's goal was to create a community as well as to supply decent housing, it searched for a design that would foster a community spirit. The COH used common sense to find out what would attract residents to this no man's land between the Gold Coast and the high-rise slums. As one of its first steps, the church leaders had initiated a survey of 1,500 residents in both nearby Sandburg Village and Cabrini-Green Homes to discover their housing preferences. The findings indicated that tenants in such transitional neighborhoods feared hallways and elevators; and that, in buildings higher than six floors, the sense of community would be lost.[6] Although the COH now had a basic idea of what it would like to build, something more was needed before the process could really begin. William Leslie, the pastor of LaSalle Street Church and president of the COH, recalled:

> City officials indicated they would like to see us with a strong team [of advisors]. So all four of the churches chipped in $1000 each. Then we went out and got some expertise and clout.[7]

Assembling the Development Team

One of the original sponsors, Fourth Presbyterian Church on North Michigan Avenue, had become a part of the COH due to a long record of service in tutoring students from Cabrini-Green. Its congregation included wealthy and influential members who had the right connections and technical expertise that would enable the COH amateurs to learn how a real estate developer worked. Lawyer and developer Daniel Epstein, who developed River City, located just south of Chicago's downtown, was retained as the COH attorney.

Planning and development funds were granted by the Illinois Housing Development Authority (IHDA). Learning sessions were set up for community people and COH staff. Federally assisted housing developments nationwide were studied. One in Minneapolis was especially noteworthy, if only for its initial failure. When this housing development opened, it had the same mix of income levels that the COH planned to have. But rather than integrating the lower-income households with the others, the

Minneapolis development segregated them in a single high rise. This isolating strategy brought down the whole project. Eventually the buildings were "salt and peppered," economically and racially, and the new strategy proved successful.

The First Step

In 1973 COH was the only developer to express interest in the DUR-owned land. The City of Chicago welcomed the COH's initiative and readily sold seven acres of land it owned to the COH, five years after the consortium of churches had been organized. The tract's boundaries were from Wells to Franklin Streets (the "el" tracks right-of-way) and from Division to Hill Streets. The DUR's selling price was written down to $2.13 a foot for the parcel of 262,667 square feet. The total price was $559,480. The sale became the first step in the redevelopment of the entire Chicago-Orleans urban renewal area.

Crane Construction Company was chosen as the general contractor upon the recommendation of Epstein, the attorney. The Crane Company enjoyed a reputation for building successful multi-family developments and for completing them ahead of time and under budget. Equally as important was its interest in working with the COH on the concept of a planned housing community. That relationship was strengthened when Crane became a general partner with an equity position of six percent.

John Petersen, then assistant to the president of a manufacturing company and a parishioner of LaSalle Street Church, became secretary of the COH. Along with Pastor William Leslie, he performed the functions of a developer. The architect was chosen with great care since the design was seen as essential to the development's success. George Schipporeit, dean of the college of architecture, planning and design at the Illinois Institute of Technology, had already established his reputation with the creation of Chicago's Lake Point Tower. His design for the new development proved to be equally distinctive.

The Atrium Concept

Defensible space[8] became the key concept in the physical development of what came to be named Atrium Village, a housing complex of 307 units on seven acres. Two streets, North Franklin and West Elm, were closed off. One nine-story elevator building which Atrium Village sponsors called a "mid rise," adjoined clusters of three-story garden apartments. Access to the

Atrium Village

Developer: Chicago-Orleans Housing Corporation and
Crane Construction Co., general partners

Units: 307 rental units

Location: Near North Side
Wells to Franklin Streets (elevated tracks
right-of-way), Hill to Division Streets

Year of Completion:1978

Initial Rents: Studio from $235
One bedroom from $349
Two bedrooms from $390
Three bedrooms/two baths from $520

Cost of Project: $10,700,000

Financing: $9.58 million (nine percent interest and a for-
ty-year construction and permanent mortgage
loan from IHDA

$420,000 equity position by COH, Crane
Construction and a limited partnership syndi-
cated by Security Pacific Co.

Fifty to fifty-five percent of the units are rented at market rates; the rest are subsidized

Architect: George Schipporeit

Contractor: Crane Construction

elevator building and the garden apartments went through entrances that provided maximum security. Glass elevators were installed in the mid rise and were visible to all through the atrium that rose to the roof. Skylights let in natural light through all levels. Walkways on each floor, instead of the usual dismal corridors, surrounded the atrium. Tenants standing on any level could see over the balconies to other levels and the elevator. Interior landscaping and seating sections were provided in the downstairs' lobby area. Here Atrium Village would host informal meetings and social activities. Access to the outdoor swimming pool and tennis courts was be from an inner court with keys obtained from Atrium's office or security person. A social room and laundry facilities were also available. Other security arrangements were added: an around-the-clock doorman in the mid-rise building, closed circuit TV to screen visitors, computerized access cards in the clusters, smoke alarms and a sprinkler system for fire safety. The physical layout of Atrium Village did succeed in fostering a sense of security.

The Financing Package

Although the COH purchased the land just before President Richard Nixon's freeze of HUD funds in 1973, that action necessitated a two-year wait for Section 236 rental subsidies. These subsidies were necessary for ensuring the acceptance of the COH's precariously balanced arrangement for financing. Perhaps the church founders had their own kind of clout, for the Illinois Housing Development Authority (IHDA) miraculously discovered a large allocation of Section 236 funds for another housing development which never materialized. These funds were then redirected to the COH. The IHDA and the COH, however, decided to rent fifty percent of the units at market rate.

The COH entered into a financing agreement with the IHDA which would provide both interim and permanent financing, contingent on a commitment for mortgage insurance from the Federal Housing Administration. On June 28, 1974, the COH began the process to obtain an FHA commitment. A site and market analysis letter was issued by HUD in April 1975, indicating that the COH proposal was feasible. In July the COH and the IHDA filed an application for a conditional commitment from HUD. The application was delayed when HUD mistakenly applied unit mortgage limits for subsidized property to all of Atrium Village rather than just to its subsidized apartments. HUD had misunderstood the financial arrangements. A majority of Atrium Village's housing units were to be market rate rather than subsidized. As a result of HUD's miscalculation, the FHA commitment received was only $7.7 million rather than the amount needed. Only after the COH had appealed to HUD's Washington office was the insurance for a $9.58 million mortgage approved in 1976. Working at the same time with the IHDA, a state agency, and HUD, a federal department, complicated matters. Petersen, the COH secretary, recalled:

> One of the unique aspects of Atrium Village was the fact that we were working with two government agencies. There were conflicting points of view, exclusionary guidelines. Sometimes reporting procedures were different. Sometimes a procedure was permitted by one agency but disallowed by the other. Eventually we learned to weave around the restrictions, working out what was best for us. The most important thing was ensuring that early decisions were made to preclude future problems--and putting everything in writing.[9]

Reduced Vandalism

Construction proceeded smoothly after the ground breaking in 1977. According to the contractor, there was less vandalism at the Atrium Village development than on some of Crane Company's other large construction projects. Except for a snowball that broke a ground floor window, site vandalism did not take place. Perhaps, the local community sensed that Atrium Village was *their* housing development, not someone else's.

Long-lasting materials were utilized in construction. Walls and columns were constructed of poured masonry. Heating and cooling systems of good quality were installed. Balconies were extensions of the horizontal floor slab. Site placement was carefully planned. The buildings were situated asymmetrically rather than squarely north/south or east/west, for more pleasing views, and the space nearest to the elevated tracks became the parking lot. Extensive landscaping of the exterior linked it to the atrium interior.

Atrium Village's mix of 307 units included: 205 studio, one and two bedroom apartments in the mid-rise building, and 102 apartments with two, three and four bedrooms in the low-rise clusters. The larger units were for families only. No children currently live in the mid-rise. Doors opened for occupancy late in 1978. Construction was completed eight years after the COH was formed.

Tenants

For the 307 units, over 1,900 applications were received. Many applicants were residents of Cabrini-Green who would qualify for subsidized apartments as they became available. Those unable to obtain subsidized apartments were put on a waiting list. This list was then frozen. New applications have yet to be taken.

Although they did not flock to Atrium Village as did low-income applicants, middle-income apartment hunters also applied. The location was convenient, situated near downtown Chicago and the shops, restaurants, night life and recreation of the Lincoln Park and Gold Coast areas. It offered amenities comparable to other complexes, such as swimming pool and tennis courts, yet with rents on the low end of the market scale. These factors, combined with top security, all contributed to the desirability of Atrium Village. Bobbie Corbett, former Atrium Village rental manager, said:

> The upscale look of the building helped too. The people who live in the building just love it and they tell their friends. Over ninety percent of our non-subsidized tenants come in as referrals from other tenants. And do the market-rate renters worry about who is paying full rent and who is subsidized? They don't ask. They don't know who is subsidized, and they don't care.[10]

Market-rate renters continue to provide the income/racial mix of Atrium Village that makes it unique in the city. There appears to be a continuing supply of white and black professionals, many with religious motivations, who welcome the Atrium Village environment. "Whenever the number of market-rate tenants starts to decline," says Pastor Leslie, "We put an ad in the *Reader*. It never fails."[11]

While the usual standards for judging tenant suitability-- personal and credit references--proved sufficient for market-rate renters, applicants for subsidized units were scrutinized more carefully. The objective was to select applicants who would prove to be upwardly mobile. Along with routine credit checks, additional standards were developed by COH's screening committee to select the best tenants:

• Employment. Does applicant hold a job? More than one?

• Academic achievement. Do the children in the family have good grades?

• After-school supervision. Would children be adequately supervised?

• Did the household satisfy high standards of good house-keeping?

Reflections of the Developer

According to Pastor Leslie, one key to Atrium Village's success was the fact that the majority of tenants attracted to the development shared the ideal of economic and racial integration. The racial mix and physical amenities of Atrium Village encouraged a community spirit, the sense of all pulling together for this human ideal. In addition, activities were developed for senior citizens in the mid rise, and after-school programs were planned for the families living in the clusters. Consequently, Atrium Village had less of the isolation which usually keeps high-rise dwellers from knowing each other's names. Here it was easier to borrow that proverbial cup of sugar, to visit with a neighbor or to recognize the others at the swimming pool.

Community vs. Privacy

One of Atrium Villages' better known tenants is Jesse White, an Illinois state legislator. Famous for his team of gymnasts from Cabrini-Green and the nearby area, White also devotes his energies to the Atrium Village community. In 1986, for example, he obtained 300 tickets to a performance of the Ice Capades and rented buses to take Atrium Village residents to the performance.[12] White may not be the typical tenant of a housing development, of course. Not every building can be so lucky.

The experience of Frances Badger, another resident, may be more representative. A professional artist, Badger moved to Atrium Village in 1979 from a building not far away. "People are friendly here," she says, "but not too friendly. I like to socialize but I have a pretty busy schedule."[13] In that respect she is more typical of apartment dwellers, even in Atrium Village. Atrium Village is therefore uniquely positioned. It offers both privacy and community, allowing its residents to choose their mix of the two. Subsidized and market-rent dwellers alike had an option not ordinarily available in a housing development.

Despite its racial and economic mix and its physical design, Atrium Village did not achieve the heightened sense of community for which Pastor Leslie and the COH had hoped. Says Leslie:

> The tenants seem to get together for crisis management only. If there's a problem, 600 people show up. A few weeks later the tenants' group is back down to twenty-five.[14]

Three successive social directors were hired to help foster the community spirit that the COH wanted. Each of the three social directors left. Only the elderly who usually had the leisure time attended social functions. The COH finally decided it could not engineer sociability. Tenants came to Atrium Village to live, and despite the congenial atmosphere, socialization could not be imposed.

Is It Succeeding?

If tenant satisfaction is a primary indicator of a development's success, Atrium Village must be considered a success. Ask the former public housing tenants who live there or the young professionals playing a round of tennis.

Secondly, from a financial standpoint Atrium Village wins too. Vacancies are infrequent. "We are HUD's biggest supporter," said Pastor Leslie. "Our excess income is a big chunk that goes to HUD."[15] According to the agreement with HUD, any rental income earned above the stipulated basic rent level reverts to HUD. John Petersen, who served as vice-president of development for Atrium Village, summed up the COH philosophy:

> It takes the same amount of effort to do six flats as to do a hundred-unit building. Since the need for housing is so great, why not spend the time and effort doing more, rather than less?[16]

Thirdly, Atrium Village's managed integration keeps working, despite contradictory policies on the part of the federal government. Upscale renters continue to be attracted, although from time to time they have to be actively recruited. The ratio of market renters to subsidized ones, however, has dropped from sixty-four percent to fifty-five percent. Ever since Atrium Village began renting, its black occupancy has hovered around fifty-one percent. These unusual ratios ensure a precarious future for Atrium Village.

Finally, security remains good. The architectural theory of defensible space has proved effective, especially inside the atrium building. Security problems have been rare except for a few break-ins in cars in the parking lot and two serious incidents in the low-rise buildings where occupants were careless. Apartment burglaries are rare. Equally important as the low crime statistics is the physical layout of Atrium Village, whose design fosters the sense of security through a carefully designed enclosure on the one hand and high visibility on the other hand.

The surrounding neighborhood has improved noticeably. Land that sold for $5 a square foot in 1975 now goes for $40 a square foot. New high-rise apartments have been built along La-Salle Drive and Wells Street. Dr. Scholl's shoe factory at 1350 N. Wells Street was remodeled and is now Cobbler Square, a rental complex of 295 loft-type luxury apartments. Small businesses have sprung up along Orleans Street. Dry cleaners and small food markets have been opened; shops and business offices have been upgraded along Wells Street. While Atrium Village cannot take all the credit for the improvements on its periphery, its continuing presence helped stimulate new commercial and residential development.

Ironically, the success of Atrium Village put into jeopardy its opportunity to build Atrium II, an addition proposed for the adjacent DUR-owned land to the south. In the early 1970s, there was little or no interest by developers in the urban renewal land purchased by the COH. The Department of Urban Renewal was delighted that the consortium of churches had been able to put together a viable housing proposal. The DUR staff even promised the COH that it could buy the adjoining urban renewal land for a second phase.

In the 1980s, however, the situation had changed. The large, vacant parcel of urban renewal land which was to have been sold to the COH for building Atrium II was now valuable property and in great demand by other developers who did not hesitate to use their political influence. That is why the sale of this publicly owned land next to Atrium Village was delayed for several years. The COH continued its interest in the construction of additional housing that would benefit, once again, tenants of low and moderate income as well as the higher income renters who have kept moving into the area. Will the COH be able to convince the City's Department of Housing to sell this parcel to a

developer who will build housing which is racially and economically integrated? To a developer who will continue to support the
bridge, between Cabrini-Green and the lakefront Gold Coast,
which Atrium Village was successful in building and maintaining? The COH wants any new housing development which ad-
joins Atrium Village to contain some apartments which will be
affordable for families from Cabrini-Green Homes and from
nearby Town and Garden Apartments.[17] The need for affordable housing continues in the Near North Side neighborhood.
Atrium Village stands as a successful example of what can be accomplished. It remains to be seen whether the COH will be giv-
en the opportunity to take the lead once again.

Reflections of the Developer

In successfully integrating households differing in income
and race, Atrium Village achieved the bridge effect which it originally intended. But is it a model for similar housing developments? Atrium Village is a development that begs to be exam-
ined. The developer set out to provide affordable housing in a
decent environment for low-income households within the community. This goal alone presented formidable challenges. Would
the rents in newly constructed buildings far exceed the ability of
the poor to pay them? Would the development's social environment be dominated by the Cabrini-Green public housing project?
Furthermore, the developers sought to do more than provide
housing; they also wanted to make Atrium Village into a community, while improving the surrounding area in a way that would
benefit the poor who lived there.

Atrium Village's sponsors ultimately realized that to improve
both the housing and the living environment for those in poverty, they would have to integrate the poor with the more affluent.
This was not an original insight; others had reached similar con-
clusions. But while some housing programs sought to improve
the environment of the poor by moving them into middle-income
neighborhoods and suburbs (e.g., public housing on scattered
sites), the COH turned the idea around and said, "Let's bring
more prosperous renters into our neighborhood. That way we
won't lose our own good church-goers."

Housing Families with Children

Necessity, opportunity and idealism converged as the COH's
vision for Atrium Village came into focus. Its housing would
demonstrate to the city how the poor and the prosperous could

live together in harmony and community. From this overall goal flowed a series of insights now embodied in Atrium Village. The architecture of defensible space provided safety and security in the "no man's land" situated between a giant public housing project and the Gold Coast. Families with children were housed in the clustered low rises while single and married adults lived in the mid rise.

The advantages of Atrium Village's location were deftly exploited. "Near North, Near Everything" was the slogan as the COH obtained acceptance of the ideals that inspired the development. The ideal of harmony amidst diversity bonded various economic, racial and age groups. Atrium Village remains a visual delight. It displays a safe and attractive environment simultaneously for low-and middle-income households. It ensures that the remaining urban renewal land will be used for further residential development. It has effectively built a bridge between two worlds in close physical proximity, but whose social distance is vast.

NOTES

1. Harvey Zorbaugh, *The Gold Coast and the Slum* (University of Chicago Press, Chicago, 1929).

2. Elizabeth Lassar, "Urban Renewal and the Development Process," an unpublished paper at the Law School of Northwestern University (1976), footnote 181.

3. Chicago Department of Urban Renewal, *Redevelopment Plan for Slum and Blighted Area Redevelopment: Project Chicago-Orleans*, Chicago, 1968, revised 1972.

4. Chicago-Orleans Housing Corporation, "A Narrative of Chicago-Orleans Housing Corporation and Atrium Village," submitted to HUD National Awards Competition.

5. As quoted in Ed Marciniak, *Reclaiming the Inner City* (National Center for Urban Ethnic Affairs, Washington, D.C., 1986), p.126.

6. University of Illinois poll of 1500 Sandburg Village and Cabrini-Green residents, 1968.

7. William Leslie, interview January 1986.

8. Oscar Newman, *Defensible Space: Crime Prevention Through Urban Design* (Macmillan Publishing Co., New York, 1973).

9. John Petersen, interview January 1986.

10. Bobbie Corbett, interview January 1986.

11. William Leslie. The *Reader* is a free, weekly newspaper oriented towards young, urban professionals living near Chicago's lakefront.

12. Frances Badger, interview January 1986.

13. Frances Badger.

14. William Leslie.

15. William Leslie.

16. John Petersen.

17. William Leslie.

5

Evergreen-Sedgwick Apartments

Tenant selection is the key to success in any development. Without good tenant selection you are doomed.--William Moorehead

Where do families find safe and decent housing in a neighborhood whose social environment is dominated by Cabrini-Green Homes, Chicago's most notorious public housing project? The neighborhood in this case is the Lower North Side, the western sector of Chicago's Near North Side whose lakefront edge is conspicuous for its wealth.

The Setting

The Cabrini-Green housing project in the mid 1960s comprised seventy-eight buildings (twenty-three of them high rises), 3,600 apartments and 20,000 official residents. Cabrini-Green's residents lived in poverty, striving to exercise control over their lives. Most households were on public aid and fatherless. Seventy percent of the residents were under seventeen years of age. Crime, gangs, teen-age pregnancy and welfare dependency were endemic.[1]

Even before the arrival of the Cabrini-Green high rises following World War II, the Lower North Side had been immortalized as a "slum" by sociologist Harvey Zorbaugh in his classic

1929 study,*The Gold Coast and the Slum*. The area was shabby, unhealthy and dangerous even then. There was, however, one major difference between the Lower North Side then and the Lower North Side after Cabrini-Green was built. Before that time it had an identity; it was a neighborhood that inspired some loyalty. After public housing arrived, the area's neighborhood life was devastated.

The Lower North Side slum periodically pricked the conscience of the city. During the 1930s and later, several giant, private initiatives were taken to redeem the area. Some examples were: the construction of the 628-unit Marshall Field Garden Apartments, the establishment of Montgomery Ward & Company's corporate headquarters, and the construction of the massive Merchandise Mart at the area's southern border along the Chicago River. In the 1940s the Cabrini-Green public housing project itself was viewed as a municipal initiative that would regenerate the area by dismantling the historic and privately owned slum.

By the 1960s the blight caused by Cabrini-Green was intensified by the influx of low-income black migrants from the rural South. Deterioration began to spread northward into the neighboring community of Lincoln Park and east toward the Gold Coast. This new threat prompted frantic efforts by government officials, institutions and community leaders to build "urban breakwaters to hold back the menacing tide of deterioration."[2] The City of Chicago launched massive urban renewal projects, several in the area between Cabrini-Green and the Gold Coast, and the others in Lincoln Park. These eventually halted the spread of blight and, in fact, stimulated a counterattack.

While earlier attempts to improve the area had simply failed or fallen short of expectations, the introduction of public housing on a grand scale sent the neighborhood into a rapid, downward spiral resulting in a desperate state of affairs by the mid 1960s. The housing had deteriorated; the schools were in shambles; city services were almost non-existent; and upwardly mobile residents who could escape did so. The neighborhood was so shattered that it had lost its historic identity.[3] The Cabrini-Green presence now dominated the entire area.

While church leaders, all housing novices, were planning an Atrium Village just east of Cabrini-Green Homes and south of Division Street, another amateur, William Moorehead, was looking for ways to improve the neighborhood lying just north of the

Evergreen-Sedgwick Apartments

Developer: Near North Development Corporation

Units: Eighty-four walk-up apartments for rent, in
           five clustered buildings four stories high

Location: Near North Side Community

           Between Sedgwick and Cleveland Streets,
           Goethe and Evergreen Streets

Year of Completion: 1978

Cost of Project: $2.4 million

Initial Basic Rent: $185 for a one-bedroom apartment
                     $224 for a two-bedroom apartment
                     $255 for a three-bedroom apartment

Financing: Construction loan: Illinois Housing Develop-
           ment Authority

           Mortgage banker: McElvain Reynolds Com-
           pany with HUD insurance using the Section
           236 rental subsidy program. Eighty percent
           of the units had low base rents made possi-
           ble by the subsidized interest rate on the
           mortgage. The rest of the units carried even
           deeper rent subsidies for households with
           very low incomes.

Architect: Environment Seven

Contractor: Tripco Construction

public housing project.   Moorehead, a local civic leader, described the Lower North Side as it was in 1964 when he and
other residents formed a new community organization, The
United Friends:

> People were moving out because of the housing. Even people
> who wanted to live here moved. Many of the houses were owned
> by absentee landlords who just drained them, then left them for
> the City to tear down. There was no new construction. We were
> surrounded by vacant property. The neighborhood was becoming
> a vast wasteland. We took a look to see how we could keep the
> good residents in the area. We wanted to save the Lower North.
> [4]

The Developer's Goals, Obstacles and Strategies

In the context of neighborhood devastation, spreading blight
and frantic efforts to contain the blight, residents of what was
left of the original Lower North Side rallied to improve their situation. Moorehead, employed at the time as a data clerk at Swift
& Company, was a resident who saw his neighborhood dying
and thought that something could be done to resuscitate it. Here
is his assessment of the task confronting TUF in the l960s:

> There wasn't much decent housing left in the neighborhood, and
> people were being forced to leave. This was where I lived, and
> where I wanted to raise my kids. I got involved on a volunteer
> basis in trying to do something about it.[5]

> What we set out to accomplish was to preserve the community
> for those families and individuals who wanted to remain in the
> Near North Side....We saw our community being destroyed, our
> leaders were moving out. The upwardly mobile up and moved![6]

In 1964, The United Friends (TUF) launched a program to
make the neighborhood more livable for families who wanted to
remain. TUF's agenda included housing, jobs, schools, improved community services and welfare rights.The area it served
ran from Division Street to North Avenue, and from Wells to
Halsted Streets.

From 1964 to 1968 not much was accomplished by TUF.
Moorehead continued to work for Swift & Company. In 1968,
however, TUF received a grant from Chicago Commons Asso-

ciation, the agency which was to become its primary mentor and benefactor. The grant was intended to help TUF develop a housing program. What resulted was the formation of the Near North Development Corporation (NNDC) as a not-for-profit vehicle to build good housing for neighborhood residents of low and moderate income and, by so doing, to spark the revitalization of the community. Three years later, in 1971, Moorehead went to work full time for the NNDC as its executive director.

The History of the Development Process

Short on confidence but long on hope, the NNDC set its sights on building housing for the families in the neighborhood which TUF had identified as its turf. The NNDC's leaders chose a deteriorated section of the neighborhood, three blocks northwest of the site proposed for Atrium Village. This site, they felt, was most likely to persuade the City's Department of Urban Renewal to acquire the property and resell it to them. The target blocks lay between the Cabrini-Green public housing project and the deteriorating Town and Garden Apartments, a large private development with 628 apartments. The site's special advantage was that it would require little displacement of existing residents.

The NNDC approached the City of Chicago about designating the site as "slum and blighted" in order to establish an urban renewal program under which the City could assemble the land, demolish existing structures, and sell the land to the NNDC at a marked-down price. While not very confident of the NNDC's ability to carry out a development project, the City's Department of Urban Renewal was nevertheless supportive of the NNDC's goals. In addition, no one else had expressed an interest in improving the site.

With the urging of TUF and the NNDC, the Department of Urban Renewal approved the "Evergreen-Sedgwick Redevelopment Plan" in November 1969. The plan called for building housing for families with low and moderate incomes that would serve the needs and desires of local residents. By June 1970 the City Council had approved the Department's designation of the area as "slum and blighted" and authorized the Department of Urban Renewal to acquire the land. The City proceeded to acquire the nine acres and cleared 1.6 acres for the NNDC's first housing development. The NNDC bought the land for seventy-five cents a square foot; today the land value is estimated at more than $10 a square foot.

Consistent with its ideals of community-planned housing, TUF members asked local residents what kinds of housing they would like to see built and what they could afford. This home-spun survey, assessing housing needs through personal contact with neighborhood residents, set the NNDC on the right track in the eyes of the community. No opposition to the housing materialized.

By this time the NNDC had gained the interest and the respect of corporate and other backers. Grants and technical assistance came from the Oscar Mayer Foundation (the Mayer meatpacking plant was near the site, and some of its workers might live in the development), the Joyce Foundation and the Continental Illinois National Bank. Additional assistance came from the *Chicago Sun-Times,* Sears, Roebuck and Company, Continental Assurance, Carson, Pirie, Scott and Company and Commonwealth Edison.

A key supporter of the development was Allison Davis, a young public interest attorney who volunteered his services. Referring to Moorehead, Davis commented:

> I thought he was interesting. He had no skills that related to real estate. His family lived here, and he kept saying he wanted to bring back the neighborhood. We were going in for urban renewal status, and he was supporting Alderman William Singer in the Democratic primary against Mayor Daley. We didn't get the land for two more years.[7]

Moorehead began to assemble his development team. Allison Davis became the attorney. McElvain Reynolds Company, with its experience in obtaining FHA 236 financing, was selected as mortgage banker. Mentor-like support for the novice developer came from Ron Laurent at McElvain Reynolds. (Laurent was later to head the Government National Mortgage Association during the administration of President Jimmy Carter.) Tripco became the construction contractor, and an architectural firm was found.

The concept of walk-up, rental housing that would engender a feeling of neighborliness began to take shape in the developer's mind. The Evergreen-Sedgwick Apartments took final form when a $1.5 million loan application was submitted to the U.S. Department of Housing and Urban Development (HUD) in early 1972 under the Section 236 rental subsidy program. The NNDC hit its first roadblock when it was discovered that new federal rules prohibited the risky expenditure of federal funds for housing families with low and moderate incomes in close proximity to existing concentrations of low-income housing. Without an invitation, Cabrini-Green was back in the picture. The NNDC persuaded HUD to bend its rule by pointing out the site's proximity to the Lincoln Park and the Gold Coast communities.

HUD issued a feasibility letter to the NNDC in August 1972, but the financing was temporarily derailed when President Nixon placed a moratorium on all federal housing programs in January 1973. It took another several months for HUD to determine that the Evergreen-Sedgwick proposal was exempt from the moratorium because it had already received a feasibility letter. Finally, in November 1973 HUD issued to NNDC a conditional commitment in the amount of $2 million.[8]

During this same period the NNDC encountered another set of delays, this time in land acquisition. Although the City had earlier awarded 1.6 acres to the NNDC, federal funds for urban renewal were being withheld from the City by HUD. HUD's dispute with the City was over the City's failure to identify scattered public housing sites in accordance with a 1971 court settlement. The City ultimately used funds from an issuance of general revenue bonds to acquire the site in 1974.[9]

The delays during the 1972-1974 period coincided with a sharp upturn in construction costs, which was largely attributable to the sudden rise in oil prices. By the time the project was put back on track, its original cost estimates were obsolete. Efforts to redesign the project to trim costs were beyond the ability of the original architects that the NNDC had employed. Hence, the NNDC brought in a new firm, Environment Seven.

Even with a new architectural firm and various economies in design, the housing development would now cost $2.4 million. In September 1975 the NNDC had to go back to HUD with a third version of its proposal To HUD's credit, it was understanding about the difficulties that the NNDC had encountered,

Evergreen-Sedgwick Apartments

and in January 1976 it approved the revised application for $2.4 million. For once timing was in the NNDC's favor, because shortly thereafter HUD discontinued its Section 236 program.

Ground was finally broken on November 29,1976. Approximately one year later, five low-rise buildings were completed. Over 1,000 applications were taken for the 84 units, presenting both a problem and an opportunity. The problem, of course, was that so many people in need of better housing had to be turned away. Twenty percent of the units had deep rent subsidies. The opportunity that presented itself was that Moorehood could be very selective about occupants. It was the tenant selection process that Moorehead devised that eventually distinguished Evergreen-Sedgwick Apartments.

Exemplary Tenant Selection

With more than ten times as many applicants as apartments, the NNDC was in a position to insist on rigorous standards for occupancy. Tenant selection became a major priority for it was linked to the purposes of the undertaking in the first place: to develop affordable housing for low-income families, and to provide a living environment insulated from the social ills of Cabrini-Green Homes.

Moorehead and his team had to be certain they did not import the social atmosphere of Cabrini-Green into the Evergreen-Sedgwick Apartments. As a native of the area, Moorehead knew the people he was dealing with, and he was determined to screen out tenants who were trouble prone. He recalled:

> People got the idea that anyone who applies here is supposed to be accepted, because it's subsidized housing. But we have a commitment to maintain sound and decent housing. We ask people to present their case for being here.[10]

Moorehead set up a stringent screening procedure for applicants. In addition to the applicants demonstrating a good credit rating, their housekeeping at the current residence had to pass a rigorous inspection. A personal interview with the head of the household followed, as well as one with the applicant's children. Moorehead considered the ability to control children's behavior to be essential. Such social control would be stronger if the housing manager also established a relationship with resident children. Moorehead felt that highly qualified tenants were so critical to the development's success that he carried out this function himself rather than delegating it. Since eighty percent of the tenants paid conventional rents, tenant selection became crucial to the development's success.

In the final group of eighty-four families, approximately sixty percent came from the immediate neighborhood. Another ten percent were former residents of the neighborhood who desired to return. The remaining thirty percent were newcomers to the area.

The ongoing management of the housing complex was as rigorous now as the screening process was then. Much of the burden for rule enforcement was placed upon the tenants themselves who were held responsible for their behavior, as well as that of their children and their guests. Tenants were urged to report promptly the misbehavior of others to the management. Loud radios were prohibited, as was loitering. Rules were enforced, and management did not hesitate to evict troublemakers. The NNDC took its responsibilities seriously. Moorehead notes: "We are an oasis in a bleak desert. We put a lot of effort into maintaining the property and running a secure project."[11]

The key, however, was not the heavy hand of enforcement by management or tenants but a community spirit which makes the development work. Neighborliness was encouraged from the start, with a group orientation of all tenants. Mandatory meetings with all tenants present were convened twice a year by management, in the spring to orient everyone to the demands of a Chicago summer and again in the fall to anticipate winter. Once each year, a family picnic was held on the grounds for all residents, with entertainment, games and refreshments.

The strict rules of behavior, tempered by the experience of neighborliness, were respected and appreciated by the tenants. During the first ten years fewer than twenty families left. At least two were evicted. Some that moved out bought homes of their own. Low turnover provided evidence that the development's continued attractiveness remains undiminished, and that rapport between tenants and management continues to flourish.

Effect on the Area and Market

What was the most immediate impact of the Evergreen-Sedgwick Apartments on the local housing market? It further inspired Moorehead and the Near North Development Corporation to go forward with the second and third phases of their housing development. Only 1.5 acres of the nine-acre urban renewal site had been used. Phase II called for a 100-unit, eleven-story high rise for senior citizens and the handicapped (Evergreen Towers). Phase III called for eighty-four apartments distributed among eight low-rise buildings, each two and one-half stories high (Evergreen Terrace Apartments).

Evergreen Towers was completed in 1981. This $4 million project utilized a direct loan from the U.S. Department of Housing and Urban Development (Section 202 program). All 100 units carried Section 8 rental subsidies. Land was obtained from the Chicago Department of Urban Renewal for $1.25 per square foot.

In 1983 Evergreen Terrace Apartments rounded out the complex with an attractive cluster of two and one-half story apartment buildings. Again, many more people applied for the eighty-four units of subsidized Section 8 housing than could be accommodated. As with its predecessors, the housing in Phase III was built on urban renewal land purchased from the Department of Urban Renewal.

A noteworthy consequence of the entire Evergreen-Sedgwick development was the real estate lesson it taught to black property owners. Black owners of housing in the neighborhood emerged to form their own organization, the Near North Property Owners Association. Through this organization, they sought to protect and enhance their real estate investment and to take advantage of the renovation movement moving south from Lincoln Park into the Lower North Side area. The NNDC's Evergreen-Sedgwick housing complex became an anchor.

This new association of property owners had to add another concern to their agenda. While fears about the ominous environment of the Cabrini-Green housing project had subsided, a new threat was at their doorstep. The Town and Garden Apartments, formerly known as the Marshall Field Garden Apartments, had degenerated during the 1970s into the city's largest privately owned slum. This 628-apartment complex of ten five-story buildings (without elevators), lying just north of the Evergreen-Sedgwick Apartments, had become the neighborhood's most visible trouble spot. Despite the threatening presence of Town

and Garden Apartments, the physical appearance and the social
environment of Evergreen-Sedgwick Apartments remained un-
scathed, attributable in great part to Moorehead's painstaking efforts with tenants.

Reflections of the Developer

In 1968 when Moorehead and the Near North Development
Corporation started to work, they had two goals in mind: one
was to build housing of high quality for the neighborhood's lower-income residents; the other was to spark a determination
among the area's landlords and homeowners to improve their living environment. Moorehead's sentiments about the NNDC's
efforts to achieve these goals evolved through the years, as reflected in this series of comments:

> The ground breaking was just about the best thing that ever hap-
> pened to me. It was a tremendous feeling, after eight years of
> waiting for it to happen.[12]

> When I started, I thought a year later you would be able to see
> something tangible. I found that just wasn't true. When I start-
> ed, I didn't know anything about housing except that people lived
> in it. I had to learn about programs and resources and how to go
> out and find them and make them work.[13]

> We're going to build some more apartments, but I know we don't
> have the resources to save this neighborhood for all the people
> who live here now.[14]

> It's not a matter of race. It is just economics that counts. Poor
> people, by definition, don't have resources, and we know the peo-
> ple with resources will come here eventually, probably pretty
> soon.[15]

> I think the success of these developments shows two things.
> There are people in this area who are responsible tenants; and
> there are owners who are interested in their tenants. These two
> factors make rental housing environments in this neighborhood
> that are as good as any others in the city.[16]

> Nobody thought we would stick with the project as long as we
> did. But we thought that what we planned would have an impact.
> And now I think that what we have done has called a halt to this
> community's downslide.[17]

In a 1986 interview Moorehead displayed unequivocal satisfaction with the NNDC's accomplishments. He expressed pride for having provided an alternative housing environment for the many households who may otherwise have left the area entirely. He lamented only his inability to accommodate many more families. Moorehead also took pride in the sense of community that developed among the residents of the Evergreen complex: the fact that its residents know each other, get along with each other and help one another. He said:

I always wanted to build a community that is socially, racially and economically mixed. All-poor communities won't work. I see that happening now.[18]

With regard to the NNDC's second goal of sparking a wider community revitalization, his feelings were ambivalent. On the one hand, he expressed satisfaction that through developments such as Evergreen-Sedgwick Apartments, lower-income families shared in revitalization and prosperity normally enjoyed only by higher-income groups. On the other hand, he feared that the revitalization occurring at the neighborhood's edges, combined with the improvement of the neighborhood's core, could cause his Lower North Side to become an extension of Lincoln Park. His neighborhood could become so exclusive that it would force out its lower-income residents.

In retrospect, Moorehead chuckled at the plunge he took as an idealistic amateur and at his on-the-job education in housing development. He expressed appreciation to mentors like Ron Laurent and Allison Davis who shared their experience and provided him the guidance he desperately needed.

Moorehead's professional progress was attested to by the success of his developments. His expertise was being recognized elsewhere. He was brought in as a consultant to Village Management for its housing development at 47th Street and South Drexel Avenue in Chicago's Kenwood community. Subsequently, the Evergreen-Sedgwick tenant selection process was installed there. The Voice of the People in Chicago's Uptown community also relied upon the NNDC's tenant selection system in the rehabilitation and rental of several multi-family buildings.

While Evergreen-Sedgwick Apartments may have been viewed as an experiment by outsiders, it was not so seen by

Moorehead and the NNDC. Most inner-city leaders already know that many of their neighbors, though poor, were responsible people. Given a chance to rent in a well-supervised and well-maintained apartment building, such housing applicants would prove to be good tenants, assets to the development. In this respect, the NNDC's success with the Evergreen-Sedgwick Apartments became a lesson only for doubters.

NOTES

1. Ed Marciniak, *Reclaiming the Inner City* (National Center for Urban Ethnic Affairs, Washington, D.C., 1986), p.58. An analysis of the history and future of Chicago's Lower North Side.

2. Ed Marciniak, p.113.

3. Dorothy Collin, "From wasteland to new housing: A dying community that wouldn't," *Chicago Tribune* (December 14, 1976), Section 1, pp. 1 and 18. A report on the development of Evergreen-Sedgwick Apartments.

4. Dorothy Collin, p.1.

5. Delia O'Hara, "Low-rent units completing Near North turnaround," *Chicago Sun-Times* (November 11, 1983), p. 38. An article quoting William Moorehead on the accomplishments of the Near North Development Corporation and the changing nature of the neighborhood.

6. William Moorehead, interview January 27, 1986.

7. Delia O'Hara, p.39.

8. Elizabeth Lassar, "Urban Renewal and the Development Process,"unpublished paper at the Law School of Northwestern University (1976), p.66.

9. Elizabeth Lassar, p.64.

10. Delia O'Hara, p.39.

11. Ed Marciniak, p.141.

12. Dorothy Collin, p.18.

13. Dorothy Collin, p.18.

14. Robert Suro, "Cabrini to Gold Coast: Bridging the gap," *Chicago Tribune* (February 5, 1978), Section 1, p.1. An article in which Moorehead describes the bridging effect of the Evergreen-Sedgwick Apartments.

15. Robert Suro, p.1.

16. Delia O'Hara, p.38.

17. Delia O'Hara, p.39.

18. William Moorehead, interview September 19, 1986.

6

Monroe-Leamington Manor

Our goal is to create an affordable, livable, just community.--Mary Nelson

It was an eyesore. The four-story building, looming from the northeast corner of Monroe Street and Leamington Avenue in Chicago's South Austin community, contrasted sharply with adjacent well-kept buildings. Not fully occupied, its apartments were spattered with graffiti; litter and debris provided nests for rodents. Those walking by were as depressed by the sight as were the real estate values which the building depreciated along this residential street. Clearly, the community deserved better.

It was a familiar dilemma. Gut and renovate? Displace tenants and charge higher rents? Wait for a guardian angel? Or take things into one's own hands? The solution involved the last alternative--and with just a touch of a guardian angel.

The Setting

South Austin is a distinctive segment of Chicago's largest community, known as Austin, which lies at the western border of the city, adjoining the suburb of Oak Park. In 1960 South Austin's occupants were 100 percent white. Well-built single-family homes and small apartment buildings, direct "el" transportation to the Loop and large churches (mostly Catholic) had made the area a popular spot for Italians, Irish, Germans and Poles moving westward from the congested neighborhoods nearer Chicago's downtown.

In the 1960s, however, the rapid influx of black families from the neighboring community of Garfield Park to the west began changing the racial complexion of South Austin. In 1966, for example, the Chicago Board of Education decided to make Austin High School a model of racial integration. Suddenly, as Father Francis Phelan, pastor of Austin's Resurrection Church, recollected, "We had 150 real estate brokers raping the neighborhood."[1] Between 1966 and 1970, no less than148 blocks in South Austin changed precipitately from white to black. Prospective black buyers were escorted into the area, while white buyers were steered elsewhere. The rioting that accompanied Dr. Martin Luther King's assassination in 1968 took place in the adjoining community of West Garfield Park. South Austin's population went from 100 percent white in 1960, to twenty-five percent white in 1970, to two percent in 1980. The racial blockbusters had won.

For a while, the prospect of total racial transition was not so obvious. During this interval, the Organization for a Better Austin (OBA) tried to stave off the inevitable. This community group was organized in the 1960s by Tom Gaudette, a protege of Saul Alinsky. Local Catholic churches were the major sources of financial support for this activist organization with a black and white membership. The OBA's tactics, following Alinsky, were highly confrontational and controversial, yet it effectively organized and mobilized a broadly based segment of the community to strive for stablity and racial integration. In the good fight against unscrupulous real estate brokers, slumlords, redlining financial institutions and insurance companies, the OBA won many battles but lost the war. Except for a small, historic section of Central Austin, resegregation by blacks had won, and racial integration had lost. The final blow was delivered to the OBA when it was discovered that its young black president was an undercover agent for the Chicago Police Department's "red squad."

High unemployment among young black males, a high proportion of families headed by women on welfare, poor public schools, skyrocketing crime rates, deteriorating apartment buildings and poor city services plagued South Austin in the 1970s, even more than in most Chicago communities. For the Austin

area as a whole in 1980, there were 358 boarded-up buildings.
[2] As a result of abandonment, arson and demolition, hundreds
of apartments vanished each year.

At the same time, however, the new black residents did not
give up on their community. South Austin still had the same
amenities that had attracted people in earlier decades. The basic
housing stock, though deteriorating in many cases, remained sol-
id. Public transportation was still excellent via the "el." And the
legacy of the OBA was a highly organized and involved community.

One of South Austin's dedicated community groups was Bethel New Life, a community organization formed in 1979 by
members of Austin's Bethel Lutheran Church at 130 North Keel-
er Avenue. When other urban churches were following their
white, middle class congregations to the suburbs, Bethel Lutheran took a different route. It decided to stay and work with the
community as it was being reconstituted. Bethel Lutheran soon
found out that Sunday services and socials for senior citizens
were not enough for the new black residents.

Surveys showed that crime was the prime concern of South
Austin's residents. But crime, if not an unsolvable problem,
was difficult to tackle directly. The second major concern cen-
tered on the deterioration of the community's housing stock. As
its first commitment to serve the community, Bethel New Life
sought to ensure decent housing for neighborhood residents by
establishing Bethel Housing, a non-profit arm for housing development. Bethel Housing was inspired by the words of Isaiah,
"You will be known as the people who rebuilt the walls, who re-
stored the ruined houses."

Developer's Goals, Obstacles and Strategies

While Bethel Housing's goal was to create an affordable, livable, just community, it sought to do so without becoming an all-
powerful "Big Brother." It did not want to play the role of a typical landlord. Housing would be improved only with the active
support of the people who lived there or nearby."Own Their
Own" and "SHARE in the Solutions Through Investments" became Bethel Housing's mottoes. As a consequence, Bethel
planned to provide housing on a cooperative basis to people with
lower incomes so that they would share ownership of the real
estate. The housing would be rehabilitated property or new

construction made possible through the efforts of the residents themselves.

Sweat Equity

The notion of self-help sounds impressive, of course. But it can become just so much rhetoric if not expressed within the actual development process. After considering several alternatives, Bethel Housing came up with a plan that seemed workable. It sought to lower construction costs through the residents' own labor and to keep maintenance expenses low through the residents' strong identification with the building. Furthermore, resident involvement in the development process would build pride of ownership and generate cooperation among the occupants. In place of rents, "monthly occupancy charges" or assessments would pay the expenses of operating the cooperative: heat, janitorial services, management, taxes, insurance, common utilities, reserve funds, repairs, maintenance, and payments of principal and interest on any mortgage for the entire building.

Three goals were identified for the plan to achieve housing ownership for families of low and moderate incomes:

• affordable housing, community spirit and pride of ownership through "sweat equity";

• mutual support through cooperative ownership; and

• continued affordability through a "limited equity" mechanism.

Resident participation was the guiding principle in the renovation and management of this cooperatively owned building. The future occupants' sweat equity, representing their contributed time and labor, would reduce the size of the down payment and make home ownership more realizable for low-income households. Sweat equity was more than the simple equation of X work+Y dollars = Z apartment. It balanced legal, economic, social and organizational considerations to make the development feasible and the system fair. It set specific conditions for membership along with the contribution of labor by tenants-to-be.

While economic advantages were paramount in cooperative projects, the social aspects were also important. The cooperative idea was developed in 1844 by the Rochdale Pioneers in England to cope with the unequal distribution of wealth in English society.[3] The Rochdale Pioneers initially opened a store and then expanded into manufacturing and services. Membership was open to those who wished to educate themselves so that they could take control of their economic destiny. The Rochdale principles that Bethel Housing would try to follow were: 1) open membership regardless of race, religion or political affiliation; 2) democratic control by members; 3) limited return on member equity, emphasizing non-profit goals so that investment income would not become a member's primary purpose; 4) expansion of services; 5) education of members; and 6) cooperation with other cooperatives.[4]

What, then, were Bethel Housing's expectations? If tenants provided part of the labor needed to rehabilitate the building, the cost of housing would be lowered and their living situation would be substantially improved. At the same time Bethel Housing hoped that the social beneifts would help achieve its urban ministry's goal of an "affordable, livable, just community." [5] New leaders would emerge from the community; skills would be learned, including those of tenant management; and tenants would become good neighbors. Finally, were the development to be successful, Bethel Housing could go on to rehabilitate similar buildings in the community.

Cooperative Ownership

Anticipating several cooperative housing developments, Bethel Housing designed an experimental cooperative which had an expandable "scattered site" capability of approximately 100 housing units. These scattered buildings were to be unified under one legal structure, Bethel Cooperative Housing. In choosing this model, Bethel sought to combine the financial stability found in individual co-op buildings with the advantages of pooled assets and financial leverage, common in larger developments.

As the not-for-profit sponsor/developer, Bethel Housing would have ultimate control of the cooperative's board until five years had passed or 100 units had been constructed, whichever came first. During this "interim development period" Bethel Housing would be ultimately responsible for all aspects, both financial and physical, of the development. It would, however, begin delegating this responsibility to cooperator-tenants, with the opportunity to step back into the picture later if the development fell into trouble during the initial five years.

Limited Equity

In order to control the resale price of rehabbed, cooperative units, the rules of a "limited equity cooperative" were employed: a limit is placed on the appreciation of individual shares. In the case of the Monroe-Leamington building, the appreciation was limited to six percent annually of the cash down payment. The down payment required on the resale of a rehabilitated unit to a new owner would be the appreciated amount. This rule restrained a unit's resale value from escalating beyond the reach of low-income households who wished to join the cooperative at a later date when an original member moved out. This feature also served to discourage ownership solely for investment purposes.

Bethel Housing's first choice for a housing cooperative was the neighborhood eyesore, the large corner apartment building at 5096-98 West Monroe Street just a few blocks from Bethel Lutheran Church. Once attractive, it had deteriorated to the point where some apartments were vacant and all were in disrepair. The building was acquired by Bethel Housing for $34,500 in 1980 with a grant from the City of Chicago's Department of Housing. The challenge now was to rehabilitate it so that it would continue to be affordable to people of modest incomes--within the framework of sweat equity, limited equity and cooperative ownership.

A History of the Development Process

Sweat equity became the key word. Experts from the Urban Homesteading Assistance Board, a New York group providing assistance to cooperative housing developments, were among those consulted in the formative stages. Successes and failures of other co-op developments were studied. Bethel New Life, along with other local community groups, then tried to convince the U.S. Department of Housing and Urban Development to fund a sweat equity demonstration project in Chicago. The building they targeted, as might be expected, was the Monroe-Leamington property.

When HUD agreed, the Chicago Rehab Network, a local federation of not-for-profit housing developers, acted as the coordinating agent for the demonstration program and for the agencies involved in it. It provided technical expertise when needed and acted as the conduit for the federal financing.

Monroe-Leamington Manor

Developer: Bethel New Life

Units: Sixteen co-op apartments for sale

Location: South Austin Community
                  5096-98 West Monroe

Year of Completion: 1983

Cost of project: $370,048

Initial Cooperator's Monthly Occupancy Charges:
                  $150 monthly for one bedroom
                  $200 monthly for two bedrooms
                  $250 monthly for three bedrooms

1986 Cooperator's Monthly Occupancy Charges:
                  $185 monthly for one bedroom
                  $235 monthly for two bedrooms
                  $285 monthly for three bedrooms

Financing: Members' equity: $19,200 (cash and labor)
                  Community Development Block Grant:
                  $34,500 for land and building
                  Mortgage loan: $135,356 at four percent un-
                  der Section 312 of the U.S. Housing Act of
                  1964
                  Rehab grants: $171,392 from the City of
                  Chicago   under the Rehabilitation of Multi-
                  unit Properties Program for correction of
                  code violations
                  Labor of six federally-funded workers:
                  $9,600 value

Architect: Bethel Housing, Inc.

Contractor:Bethel Housing, Inc.

When Bethel Housing was assembling its financing package for the Monroe-Leamington development in 1980, the special abilities of Bethel Housing's Executive Director, Mary Nelson, paid major dividends. At that time, Mayor Jane Byrne sought to renew relationships with solidly based neighbornood institutions. Bethel Housing was such as agency. The partnership between City Hall and neighborhood was translated into a multi-faceted approach to fund the Monroe-Leamington development. Working successfully with three different mayors, Nelson had demonstrated a knack for working with City Hall. As the leader of a neighborhood-based group, she knew how to cultivate good day-to-day relations with the municipal government and its various agencies for the benefit of the South Austin community. She had a vision of partnership--the City and neighborhood working together.

The Financing

In addition to the $34,500 grant from the Chicago Department of Housing to acquire the land and building, the City approved a loan of $135,356 at four percent interest from HUD under the Section 312 program. A second grant of $130,000 came from the City's program for the rehabilitation of multi-unit properties. Later, the City augmented the grant by another $41,392. To top it off, the City provided six workers, funded by a federal manpower program, to assist in the rehabilitation work. Their combined labor was valued at $9,600.

The equity to be supplied by each of the sixteen tenant-cooperators amounted to $1,200 (at least $350 of which had to be paid in cash with the balance in sweat equity at the value of $5 per hour). The combined equity, therefore, of all sixteen cooperators came to $19,200. The total project cost was $370,048, an average cost of $23,128 per apartment.

Selecting the Tenants

Early in 1981 Bethel Housing moved from concept to concrete. It would now try to put its dream into action by involving cooperator-tenants in the development process as early as possible. Bethel Housing's board members and staff made an effort to know the existing tenants personally. Housekeeping habits and the number of occupants in each apartment were checked. Credit records were verified. Of the fourteen tenants occupying the building when Bethel Housing acquired it, nine were invited to membership in the cooperative. Three declined to become members and six accepted. Of the five remaining tenants, some rejected the cooperative idea, while others were found to be un-qualified. The resident pimp was moved out, along with his "girls" and their sixteen bikes, each with its own name plate-- advertising in the South Austin style. For the ten remaining va-cancies, the new cooperator-tenants were drawn from the com-munity with the assistance of the original tenants who had agreed to join the cooperative.

Tenant Vickie Fitzgerald, president of the cooperative, ex-plained how cooperator-tenants were finally chosen:

> Tenant selection is the key to a good co-op. It takes practice and experience to learn how to read potential members. Naturally eve-ryone puts up a good front for the home visits--good housekeep-ing and so on. What we need are members who will participate in the activities of the building. If they just want to pay their fees and keep to themselves, they should stay in a rental situation, not a co-op.[6]

After selecting the cooperators, Bethel Housing attempted to ex-plain to them the ramifications of sweat equity and a limited equi-ty cooperative. How much work would be required? What would be the down payment on a member's share? Mike Rohr-beck, the Bethel New Life staff person who worked on the Mon-roe-Leamington building, said:

> It's easy to buy into the concept of sweat equity. Working to-gether, being in charge of one's own building, keeping costs low---all sound good. What we had to be careful to do was to ex-plain the real amounts of work involved. We had to be careful not to oversell the concept.[7]

The sweat equity and limited equity agreement was hammered out. Values of the construction tasks were calculated, and the cost of individual shares was determined. Rules for transfer of ownership and other policies were developed.

The Construction Phase

Actual rehabilitation of the Monroe-Leamington building be-gan in January 1981, when future occupants were given their first opportunity to invest their sweat equity. One of the more satis-fying tasks of total rehabilitation came first--the wielding of crowbar and shovel to gut the interior of the building, one vacant apartment at a time. Cooperators tore out rusted plumbing and rotted floors. Sometimes, as in the heat of battle, a little too much was removed. Once, when the construction supervisor left to purchase supplies, he returned to see eleven hardwood doors that had been diligently removed, now standing in the alley awaiting pickup. The doors were hastily retrieved and replaced on their hinges. The workers then cleaned out the basement's rubbish which had been untouched for four years.

Now the contractors came in to do the major rehabilitation. However, on-site supervisor Stanley Rushing noted:"Rehabbing is more challenging than new construction. We have to fit new technology into old design."[8] The painstaking process would eventually result in new kitchens and bathrooms, refinished floors, new storm windows, 1 1/2 inch insulation in the exterior walls and landscaping.

At the end of the working day, the major job of the cooperators was to clean up after the construction crews. The cooperators also primed and painted walls, ceilings and hallways. At this stage, an especially important role for the cooperators emerged: keeping the building secure. Although taken lightly at first, the cooperators soon realized that it was up to them to protect their own property. After thefts of construction materials, cooperators began sleeping at night in half-renovated apartments in order to guard against vandalism and theft. Not only did they successfully frighten off burglars, they actually apprehended several of them. As each new apartment became ready, the original cooperators would move in. In this way cooperators lived in the building while rehab progressed.

Irresolvable problems with the contractor soon developed. A second and then a third contractor was hired, but the quality of their work was also not acceptable. Bethel Housing then had to take over as general contractor. Referring to the difficulties with the reliability and quality of work, co-op board member, Earline Shaw, recalls:

> One of the worst problems was the "mix-up" in contractors. Some of the people had waited for a year to move in and were threatening to pull out of the agreement. They were tired of waiting for their new apartments.[9]

Monroe-Leamington Manor

As the rehabilitation took shape, however, it became easier to recruit sweat-equity labor. And the labor itself became more skilled. A recurring difficulty was the inability or unwillingness of the contractors to integrate the cooperators' sweat equity into the work schedule. Later on, construction supervisors became more creative at utilizing the new skills of the tenants. One problem arose, however. "We could have used more men," Earline Shaw admits. "Most of us were single, working women. A little more muscle would have been nice."[10]

By September 30, 1982 more than $11,300 in sweat equity had been contributed by the sixteen cooperator-occupants. Seven people had contributed their sweat-equity hours in full. Most of the rest had earned close to the figure and paid off the difference in cash at $5 per hour. The equity contribution by cooperator-tenants (cash plus sweat) totalled $19,200.

Management Roles for Cooperator-Tenants

By 1982 the cooperators were beginning to play a stronger role vis-`a-vis Bethel Housing, their prime sponsor. Of the five-member board of Bethel Cooperative Housing, three were named by Bethel Housing and two came from the building. Sitting with the rest of the board, the building residents now approved budgets and contractors and dealt with crises. But the two building representatives suddenly found themselves also taking unaccustomed responsibility for decisions concerning delinquent payments and sweat equity. Says Earline Shaw:

> We had to make some hard decisions the first two years. We were too lenient at the beginning as far as carrying charges [cooperator monthly occupancy charges] were concerned. Finally we decided to impose a $25 late fee, and this helped.[11]

The rest of the cooperator-occupants were given decision-making responsibilities through a committee system. The building committee, for instance, was given the authority to oversee maintenance of the common areas. Such cooperator-tenant involvement was in keeping with the goals of Bethel Housing. Sweat-equity skills and involvement in the management process gave cooperator-tenants a chance to take a firm hand in controlling their lives. Mike Rohrbeck points out:

> As tenants became more intimately involved in ownership, they matured a lot. By this "baptism of fire" they learned negotiation

skills, discretion in use of funds, how to manage a building.[12]

As the responsibilities of the cooperative board increased, monthly meetings became semi-monthly. "Only the officers of the co-op were required to attend these meetings," says Vickie Fitzgerald. "We didn't want everybody to burn out."[13]

By 1982 day-to-day management had been entrusted to an outside firm hired by Bethel Housing. This was in anticipation of Bethel Housing's long-range strategy for developing several cooperatives and maximizing economy of scale. Another reason for an outside firm was the need to shift the burden of dealing with reluctant or recalcitrant cooperator-occupants. Agreements on a set contribution of the sweat-equity hours were not being fulfilled by some cooperators; others had not even paid their $350 fee. The fine line to be walked among Bethel Housing, the cooperative's board, and cooperator-tenants could more easily be navigated by an outside management firm.

On April 25th, 1983 the building was dedicated in a community celebration. Along with the physical improvement of the building, its name was upgraded as well. The former eyesore at Monroe Street and Leamington Avenue was now called Monroe-Leamington Manor.

By 1985 the board of Monroe-Leamington Manor had become totally independent of its sponsor. During the interim period only two cooperator-tenants had sold their shares. In accordance with the limited equity policy, replacement tenants were able to buy into the cooperative for only $450 a share, thus proving the effectiveness of the limited equity tool for keeping housing values affordable to families of low incomes.

Effect on the Area

Monroe-Leamington Manor continues to serve as an example for redevelopment in the South Austin community. Since its completion in 1983, owners of nearby properties have made noticeable efforts to spruce up their own buildings. In addition, Bethel Housing itself came into its own with the success of the Monroe-Leamington building. It was spurred to move into more ambitious developments. A new forty-unit building for senior citizens was constructed at 4201 West Washington Boulevard. Fourteen units of in-fill housing were built on vacant lots along

Washington Boulevard. A former YMCA, constructed in 1897 for railroad workers, was rehabbed to hold the Bethel New Life Center. Bethel Housing embarked on a comprehensive plan to improve the corner of Karlov Avenue and Washington Boulevard where its office is located.

Another major housing development was the renovation of the Guyon Hotel at 4000 Washington Boulevard. Bethel Housing converted the former ten-story hotel into 124 apartments, each with one or two bedrooms. The building had received federal designation by the National Register of Historic Places, making it eligible for a tax credit when rehabilitated. By the end of 1986 Bethel Housing had been responsible for the new construction or rehabilitation of 371 housing units. In 1987 work had begun on another 197 units.

From the beginning of the renovation, a constant stream of visitors came to Monroe-Leamington Manor to see how a successful sweat-equity co-op could be organized. Bethel Housing and cooperator-tenants were asked to participate in national conferences to share their expertise. Other projects, such as those simultaneously undertaken by The Neighborhood Institute in Chicago's South Shore community, traded knowledge and encouragement with Bethel Housing.

Reflections of the Developer

Apart from providing a role model, how successful was Bethel Housing's first attempt at cooperative housing? Could success be measured solely in terms of the dollars saved through sweat equity? The $11,300 saved is a small percentage of $370,048, the total cost of the development. This is where the term "affordability" shows its relative nature. The significance of the $11,300 in contributed labor was not in the cost reduction of the entire development, but in the reduction of the cash down payment required of each cooperator-tenant. It is far easier for a poor family to provide $350 in cash as a down payment than $1,200. Sweat equity made the big difference.

Reflecting on the Monroe-Leamington development, Bethel New Life's Executive Director, Mary Nelson, feels that the success of this development encouraged Bethel Housing to start additional housing programs.Nelson notes, "We learned a lot from our first sweat equity project. Thanks to the Monroe-Leamington Manor we now proceed much more efficiently with our other efforts."[14]

Both staff and cooperator-residents admit that the development of Monroe-Leamington Manor was a learning experience in organizing a cooperative and in working with sweat equity. Bethel undertook one other sweat-equity development, the Douglas Villa Cooperative at 4350 Washington Boulevard. It was a lot easier the second time around. The rehabilitation of this 24-unit building was completed in 1985. Other cooperative cooperative developments, however, have not relied on sweat equity. For example, in the Eddie South Cooperative at 4129 Washington Boulevard, occupied in 1985, Bethel converted a thirty-unit building into fifteen cooperative apartments, where the "membership fee" was $5,000, the purchase price of the unit.

Bethel Housing's progress clearly reflects an endorsement of both the limited equity principle and the use of the cooperative form of ownership. However, the original concept of a single umbrella cooperative organization for several buildings, up to as many as 100 units, was abandoned in favor of a separate cooperative for each building, i.e. Monroe-Leamington Manor, Douglas Villa and Eddie South. The anticipated advantages of a single sponsoring cooperative did not prove practical; financing was so different for each building that it was not possible to combine them without adding more layers of bureaucracy.

Bethel Housing was pleased to prove that under the right conditions, lower-income households could gain greater control of their lives and their housing. They could not have done it on their own. They needed an institutional sponsor to support them when taking the first step. Bethel Housing provided that safety net. With Bethel Housing providing leadership and a sponsoring framework, sweat equity became a useful way for making good housing attainable for people of modest income.

Sweat equity is no panacea, however. It is hard work. Many of those involved claim they would never do it again. "It was worth it for a nice place to live, one that doesn't take all your income for rent. But I'd never do it again," said Earline Shaw. [15] And Vickie Fitzgerald says she would just as soon pay the contractors up front, and not have to depend on unreliable tenants to do the work.[16] The cooperative owners, however, do not have to "do it again." They now own their housing units cooperatively, a circumstance they admit would have been unlikely before the rehabilitation of Monroe-Leamington Manor.

Monroe-Leamington Manor was an experiment for Bethel Housing. For Bethel Housing and others it offered several lessons in the development of low-income housing. The administration and coordination of a sweat-equity program is time consuming and labor intensive in itself. The sweat-equity approach demanded herculean organizational and physical efforts by the cooperative owners of newly rehabilitated apartments and by Bethel Housing which, through Monroe-Leamington Manor, saw this as a learning experience. Bethel Housing fulfilled the prophecy of Isaiah, which Mary Nelson is fond of quoting:

> Your people will rebuild what has long been in ruins, building again on old foundations.You will be known as the people who rebuilt the walls, who restored the ruined houses.--Isaiah 58: 9-12

NOTES

1. Donald Kelly, "Profile of South Austin Community," unpublished report for The Donor's Forum of Chicago (April 1983), pp.3-4.

2. *Local Community Fact Book: Chicago Metropolitan Area* (Chicago: Chicago Review Press, 1984), p.69.

3. "What is Sweat Equity?" Urban Housing Assistance Board report (1982), pp.4-9.

4. Urban Housing Assistance Board.

5. Mary Nelson, interview March 1986.

6. Vickie Fitzgerald, interview March 1986.

7. Mike Rohrbeck, interview February 1986.

8. *City Edition*, City of Chicago Newsletter (1980), Vol. II, No.2, p.1.

9. Earline Shaw, interview February 1986.

10. Earline Shaw.

11. Earline Shaw.

12. Mike Rohrbeck.

13. Vickie Fitzgerald.

14. Mary Nelson.

15. Earline Shaw.

16. Vickie Fitzgerald.

7

Palmer Square
Apartments

*The Palmer Square Apartments development
was like seeding a cloud.*--Saul Klibanow

One neighborhood strategy for dealing with urban residential
blight is to turn the psychology of the marketplace around--by re-
juvenating the very worst buildings. The renovation of the Palmer Square Apartments in the Logan Square community was just
such an approach.

The Setting

Logan Square, on Chicago's northwest side, had for genera-
tions served as a port of entry for foreign-speaking, working-
class immigrants. Originally settled by Scandinavians and Germans, Logan Square welcomed a huge influx of Poles and Rus-
sian Jews following World War I. During the Great Depression,
a decade later, the population had reached its peak of 114,000
residents.

For the ensuing quarter of a century the population of Logan
Square decreased, as upwardly mobile immigrants and their families worked their way into less densely populated parts of the
city and suburbs. Although still graced by two tree-lined boulevards, a traffic circle around a distinguished monument marking
the 1918 centennial of Illinois and solidly constructed greystone
mansions along the boulevards, the Logan Square community

began to deteriorate rapidly between 1960 and 1970.

During the suburbanward explosion in the years following World War II, many residents moved out. Filling the vacuum was a new immigrant group. Although in 1960 there were only 569 people of Hispanic origin in Logan Square, by 1970 there were 16,000. And by 1980 there were 44,000, more than half of the community's population.

During the 1970's, the so-called urban gentry introduced itself into the community. Logan Square's spacious apartments and dowager mansions caught the attention of young professionals, including Hispanics, who were being priced out of the nearby lakefront communities of Lincoln Park and Lakeview. The latest arrivals found the quality of the housing stock and prices very attractive, as they did the ethnic mix the area still offered. The newcomers purchased prime buildings in prime locations to renovate. Though highly visible, the recently settled gentry was estimated at no more than ten percent of the population of Logan Square.

In the mid 1970s Logan Square was a whirlpool of three demographic trends: the exodus of the Eastern Europeans, the mass in-migration of Hispanics, and the arrival of the urban gentry. Several community organizations were active in Logan Square during the 1970s. Some tried to bring together the competing groups within the area under an umbrella organization. Other smaller organizations appealed to specific segments of the community, for example, the Hispanics. Consensus was not easily reached; each group felt threatened by any promotion of the other's interests. The acquisition and rehabilitation of certain buildings provoked noticeable reaction. Some Hispanics, in particular, felt that such renovation displaced their people.

A rare consensus did develop, however, around a series of eight buildings on the west side of the 2100 block of North Kedzie Boulevard. The eight buildings and their 215 rental units were considered by all to be the community cesspool. Writing in a community newspaper, reporter Sally Levin noted:

> Latinos call the buildings "el reververo," like a highly inflammable oil lamp. They were a place to stay away from, teeming with rats, drugs, prostitution, subject to frequent fires and vandalism; always, it seemed, ready to explode.[1]

Palmer Square Apartments

Developers: Palmer Square Apartments Associates: RES-
CORP   (Renewal Effort Service Corp.) and
Hispanic Housing Development Corporation

Units: 160 subsidized and market rental apartments
in six buildings

Location: Logan Square Community

2100 north on Kedzie Boulevard between
Dickens Street and Palmer Square

Year of Completion: 1980

Cost of Project: $ 6.5 million

Initial Rent: $377 for a unit with one bedroom to $553 for
a duplex unit with three bedrooms (market-
rate rents)

Financing: Construction financing : IHDA

Permanent financing: IHDA (forty-year term)

City grant from Department of Urban Renewal: $462,000

HUD Section 8 rental assistance

Architect: Swann and Weiskopf; Cabanan and Cabanan

Contractor: Nathan Linn and Son

The Organization of Palmer Square had pursued these eight buildings through housing court for many years, but their owners were able to evade neighborhood pressures to improve the properties by transferring titles. By the mid 1970s the blight emanating from the buildings began to infect the surrounding area. Adjacent property owners refrained from further investment in their own buildings, deferring maintenance and accelerating the downward spiral. Neighbors clamored to have the buildings demolished.

In 1975 the Reverend Daniel Alvarez, who was then serving as a special assistant to Illinois Governor Daniel Walker, convened a conference on housing with Hispanic groups. The conference, held in Joliet, was attended by more than 100 representatives from Hispanic communities located in different sections of the state, but mainly from Chicago. Subsequently, Alvarez reported to the Governor the results of the conference and stressed the need for an organization that would give Hispanics an opportunity to play a housing role in Chicago. The not-for-profit Hispanic Housing Development Corporation was set up in 1975, and Alvarez and attorney Eduardo Mendez became the charter members. They searched the country for an Hispanic with a background in housing and found Hipolito (Paul) Roldan in Brooklyn, New York. He was hired as executive director. The Technical Assistance Corporation for Housing was charged with providing Roldan with an additional year of training and orientation to introduce him to the Chicago scene.

Financial help came from Governor Walker, who arranged a grant of $145,000 to Hispanic Housing through the Illinois Housing Development Authority. Alvarez became the president and chairman of the board of directors of Hispanic Housing, positions which he still holds. In November 1975 Alvarez ended a two-year leave of absence from Casa Central and returned to his regular post as its executive director. Casa Central was eventually to become the largest social service agency operated by Hispanics in the United States.

With ten years of experience in the Logan Square community via his leadership of Casa Central, Alvarez brought to Hispanic Housing his concern for the worsening of housing conditions in that community. Hispanic Housing also shared a concern for the increasing gentrification of the area and for the possibility of losing Hispanics of modest income. Alvarez expressed this view:

We could see that gentrification coming....We could see that if the community did not undertake its own rehabilitation, then investors would. And by the time they were through, many of our people would not be around to see the results.[2]

Developers' Goals, Obstacles and Strategies

Hispanic Housing with its limited experience entered into a partnership with RESCORP (Renewal Effort Service Corporation), an experienced, for-profit housing agency sponsored by fifty-five savings and loan associations in Chicago to help carry out their social and neighborhood responsibilities. Their paths had crossed in 1977. RESCORP, winding down its rehabilitation of two large multi-unit housing developments in Chicago's South Shore community, was searching for a third undertaking. Hispanic Housing, on the other hand, was seeking an experienced partner from whom it could learn and which had the necessary capital resources it lacked. Saul Klibanow, president of RESCORP, was introduced to Roldan, executive director of Hispanic Housing, by Ralph Brown of the Technical Assistance Corporation for Housing, who saw the potential for a mutually beneficial partnership.

Without a specific housing site in mind and even without a neighborhood identified in advance, the two agencies explored the possibility of a temporary relationship. Both Klibanow and Roldan recall the initial circumspection of the two parties.[3] Stereotypes had to be overcome first: the "big bucks savings and loan subsidiary" versus the "socially sensitive" local development corporation. Each had a constituency with a different view of what the negotiations were all about, what their common goals should be, and who should be in charge. In addition, the Hispanic community's concerns about revitalization and displacement were being played out.

RESCORP had been formed in 1972 as part of the Chicago financial industry's response to the charges of redlining and abandonment of the inner city. Yet RESCORP was never a mere gesture. It was charged with the mission of reversing the decline of urban communities. It came fully equipped with a strategy for doing so: to create a critical mass by undertaking superior rehabilitation of strategically located residential properties. Their rehabilitation would encourage neighboring owners to rehabilitate their own residential properties.

Palmer Square Apartments

In 1977, with a broad agreement in place, the partners went shopping for an opportunity for residential rehabilitation in a declining community with Hispanic residents. Several neighborhoods were looked at, but nothing seemed right until they came across the 2100 block of North Kedzie Boulevard in the Logan Square community.

A marriage of broad purposes was worked out between RESCORP and Hispanic Housing as Roldan and Alvarez became convinced of Klibanow's sincerity and RESCORP's sensitivity towards the housing needs of modest-income Hispanics. It was agreed that all decisions would be by consensus until a property was actually acquired by the partnership. Thereafter, since RESCORP was the partner more at risk financially, it would have final word in the event of an impasse. This was a prerogative that never needed to be invoked since consensus between the partners was achieved readily.

History of the Development Process

Rehabilitation of the eight properties on North Kedzie Boulevard with 215 apartments suited the partners' purposes. The buildings were the heart of the blight besieging the Logan Square community, and the surrounding area was at least fifty percent Hispanic. The original plan called for the acquisition and rehabilitation of all eight buildings and for reducing the number of apartments to approximately 200.

The Illinois Housing Development Authority was identified as a desirable lender because of its ability, through its bonding authority, to offer construction and permanent financing at below-market interest rates. It appeared to be a potentially interested lender because of its initial support of Hispanic Housing and because of its involvement with previous RESCORP developments. Moreover, the proposed development matched the IHDA's goal of producing more housing for low-income, minority households.

A commitment from HUD for Section 8 housing assistance payments enabled the IHDA to make a $5.3 million permanent mortgage loan. The developers later sold a limited partnership interest to investors. RESCORP and Hispanic Housing each retained a one percent interest and remained as general partners. They also undertook the responsibility of managing the apartments.

The first obstacle the developers would encounter became evident as the properties were being acquired--the large amount of back taxes due. Unless the overdue taxes were reduced, the total cost of rehabilitating the buildings and the high rents that would have to be charged would be prohibitive, making the development financially unfeasible. This impediment was surmounted with the assistance of the State's Attorney who agreed to file an *in personam* suit and to negotiate a reasonable settlement with regard to back taxes. Interest and other penalties were waived.

The problem with back taxes having been resolved late in 1977, the partners proceeded to firm up financing for the Palmer Square properties. RESCORP and Hispanic Housing formalized their relationship by forming Palmer Square Apartments Associates.

The second obstacle to be faced came with the realization that not all eight buildings could be saved and rehabbed. Although the largest of the eight, a seventy-two unit building, was so deteriorated that it was vacant and scheduled for demolition, it was nevertheless salvaged in the final rehabilitation plan. To the developers' dismay, however, two other buildings were deemed structurally unsuited for rehabilitation as family apartments by the IHDA, the lender.

Paul Roldan related how an untimely transaction might well have doomed the two buildings, one of which was a common corridor building with fifty-four units which operated as a transient hotel. The developers were taking representatives of the IHDA and the City's Department of Urban Renewal on a tour of this building when a "mean looking character" appeared in the hallway carrying a bag stuffed with narcotics. Oblivious to the visitors, he proceeded to knock on an apartment door, hand the occupant the bag and take a sum of money in return. Roldan conjectured that the brazenness of the transaction may have convinced the IHDA that the best way to deal with that particular building was to demolish it and replace it with a parking lot. Another of the original eight buildings met the same fate; it too failed to meet the IHDA's standards. The loss of these two buildings with a total of fifty-six units meant a loss of significant income for debt repayment. Suddenly the financing package was short $462,000.

Fortunately, RESCORP and Hispanic Housing had a supporter within the Department of Urban Renewal, who appreciated what they were trying to accomplish. Deputy Commissioner George Stone was instrumental in arranging for a $462,000 grant from the City to cover the shortfall.

The reduction of the scale of the development not only affected the budget, but also diminished the impact the development could have on the surrounding area. Here, the element of critical mass was crucial. RESCORP, in particular, knew from experience that 200 or more units would have a significantly greater impact than 160. Although 160 units were considered to be too few in number for the purpose, they were just enough to hold the developers' interest in the project.

Quality was as crucial as scale if the developers were to be successful in having a positive influence on housing in the adjoining area. Therefore, both the work to be done and the marketing of the development would have to project the image of high quality.

The revised plan called for rehabilitation of six buildings containing 160 units and for the demolition of two buildings to accommodate a parking lot. The planned rehabilitation included structural repairs, some duplex apartments for families with children, new roofs, insulation, new interior wall surfaces, exterior sandblasting, individual heating and air conditioning, new kitchens and baths, modernized plumbing and electrical equipment, security systems, and new fixtures throughout. The concern for a public image of high quality inspired careful attention to the exteriors, visual elements such as outdoor recreation spaces, seating areas, and extensive landscaping. This was to be "life extension rehab," i.e., the remodeling was designed to last the life of the mortgage which was forty years. (The assumption was that the basic structure of old, multi-family buildings was sufficiently sound to support major rehabilitation and to assure appraisers of a useful life of at least another forty years.)

While the existing buildings contained mostly one-bedroom units, the rehabilitation plans provided for 112 one-bedroom units, thirty-seven two-bedroom units, and eleven with three and four bedrooms for large families. Rehabilitation costs were estimated at $30,000 to $32,000 per unit for interior improvements and approximately $40,000 per unit when other costs of the development were averaged in, such as the exterior work and landscaping. While the per-unit cost was considered high at the time, it was seen as worthwhile in view of the desire to establish a development that would send an encouraging word to community residents and to the local housing market. Furthermore, the federal government's Section 8 subsidy program for substantial rehabilitation would enable Palmer Square Apartments to accommodate a substantial number of low-income families.

A major challenge facing the developers was the building of a community consensus backing the development or, at the very least, ensuring its neutrality. With the diversity of groups in Logan Square, forging a consensus among supporters was not easy. The *Logan Square Free Press* described the process:

> Community support for the project was slow in coming. Some people had heard promises before and needed to be assured that this one was real. Others were suspicious of the rent subsidy program and were concerned that the project would develop public housing-type problems. Still others were certain that it was just a plan that would later be converted into condominiums for higher income folks. And finally, one group wanted the entire project to serve Latinos only.[4]

In this stage, the involvement of the locally based Hispanic Housing Development Corporation proved useful. The proposed development gradually won acceptance from such groups as the Logan Square Neighborhood Association, The Organization of Palmer Square and the board of directors of Casa Central. Alderman Richard Mell of the 33rd Ward was kept informed and consulted during this stage of the process.

What finally attracted the support of the community leaders? It was the sincerity of the development team, combined with assurances from the U.S. Department of Housing and Urban Development (HUD) and the IHDA that there would be strict tenant screening, an ethnic and income mix, and restrictions against condo conversion. Also assuaging community concern was the assurance that the new Palmer Square Apartments would be a development of high quality. In this regard, the developers' concern coincided with the community's own interest.

By late 1978, a favorable settlement had been reached on back taxes, the financing was in place, and the community was becoming increasingly supportive.The properties were then acquired by the partnership. In December 1978, approximately eighteen months after the properties had been selected by the developers, the ground breaking took place. By February 1980 one hundred units had been rebuilt and were occupied.The remaining sixty units were filled by spring. Renting the apartments was no problem at all. In view of the Section 8 subsidies, it was not surprising that the developers received three applications for every unit available.

Tenant Selection

It was in the selection of tenants that the developers encountered difficulties. In 1979 the Legal Assistance Foundation filed a lawsuit against the Palmer Square Apartments on behalf of five families, former residents of one of the buildings. The suit alleged that the families had not been given priority in the renting of the newly rehabbed apartments as was their right under both HUD and IHDA guidelines. The suit further alleged that the developers and the City of Chicago had failed to fulfill their obligations to relocate families.[5]

Without disputing the responsibilities cited, the developers explained that residents who had left prior to the acquisition of the properties, anticipating eviction because they had not paid their rent, could not now exercise their relocation rights under the Uniform Relocation Act. The five families being represented in the suit fell into that category.[6] The developers noted further that some of these families who later applied for the rehabbed units had more persons in the household than the size of the apartment would now permit. Several families had been "extended" to include eight or more people.

The dispute was settled when the developers agreed to offer a unit to each of the five plaintiffs; to amend the selection plan so as to give preference to former tenants who were clearly displaced; to make occupancy standards less restrictive; and to establish an informal review procedure for former tenants who were rejected.[7]

The selection of tenants can be a disruptive issue, especially when a major objective of the new development is to change the character of the building occupancy. The blighting impact of the eight buildings was not only due to their physical condition but to the activities of the residents as well. Many of the former tenants were themselves the source of blight, as evidenced by the drug transaction which was witnessed by the lenders. How then does a developer rid a troubled building of bad characters without unfairly penalizing responsible, low-income families at the same time? The task was especially delicate in this case because of community concern about the quality of the tenancy and the developers' commitment to screen tenants. The exasperating experience of the Palmer Square developers in trying to sort out reliable tenants was to prove valuable in RESCORP's and Hispanic Housing's future developments. In subsequent large-scale rehabilitation developments, such as the 446-unit Parkways project in Chicago's South Shore community, RESCORP assigned a full-time relocation specialist to inform tenants fully of their rights and to pre-qualify current tenants early in the process.

Out of the original 215 units distributed among the eight buildings acquired by the developers, all seventy-two units in the one large apartment building were vacant at the time the developers took title. Eighty-three existing tenants found other accommodations on their own. There remained another sixty households to be relocated. According to Klibanow, a majority of the sixty were enticed to apartments elsewhere because of the City's generous allowance of $4,000 for each household being relocated. In the end, twenty to twenty-five of the original tenants were accommodated in the new Palmer Square Apartments.[8] That left 135-140 apartments to be rented to new occupants.

A marketing strategy was developed to fulfill the developers' pledge to maintain an ethnic and income mix of responsible tenants. Brochures were printed in both Spanish and English, and both Spanish-speaking and English-speaking rental agents were hired. Display ads, communicating an image of high quality, were placed in the metropolitan press, neighborhood papers, community organization newsletters, and a Spanish-language newspaper. Flyers were distributed through churches, banks, stores, senior centers and places of employment in targeted areas. And a model apartment was available for viewing by apartment seekers.

When the development opened in 1980, the marketing goals of the developers had been met. The tenancy was distributed as follows: Hispanics (sixty percent), other whites (twenty-five percent), and blacks (fifteen percent). Initial rents were $285 for a one-bedroom unit and went as high as $550 for a four-bedroom apartment. Ten percent of the original apartments were leased at "market-rate" rents, with no subsidies.

Effect on the Area and Market

Palmer Square Apartments was Hispanic Housing's first experience in the major rehabilitation of a multi-unit property. The second large undertaking was Diversey Square Apartments, done in partnership with Crescent Development Ltd., a subsidiary of the New Frontier Development Corporation. Diversey Square Apartments, comprising 196 units in eight buildings along Diversey Parkway, is located seven blocks north of Palmer Square Apartments. In 1984 Daniel Alvarez, president of Hispanic Housing, was able to claim:

> Once that project opened [Palmer Square Apartments], it immediately began to change the way people looked at the neighborhood....Since then we have completed a second large-scale rehab. The two projects are about three quarters of a mile apart, and by now several dozen homeowners on the streets in between them have upgraded their properties as well.[9]

Alvarez pointed to other major rehab projects in the immediate area that he felt could be attributed to the momentum generated by Palmer Square Apartments: a 36-unit building on Palmer Square across Kedzie Boulevard and the 54-unit Lorrington Apartments on Kedzie Boulevard diagonally across the street from Palmer Square Apartments. He also noted the beautification along Logan Boulevard and its recent designation as an historic district.

Many feared that a housing development where apartments had Section 8 subsidies would adversely affect the local housing market. That apprehension was dispelled by a team of professors from Loyola University of Chicago. In 1983 Elizabeth Warren, Robert M. Aduddell and Raymond Tatalovich published a monograph that assessed the impact of four subsidized developments on their local markets. One of these developments was the Palmer Square Apartments. The study concluded that the "impact of subsidized housing is benign, neither a negative nor a positive factor." Moreover, in the case of Palmer Square Apartments the study found that real estate prices rose faster in the immediate area than in comparable sections of the community without rehabilitated, subsidized housing developments. The Loyola

University researchers concluded that the Palmer Square Apartments development might indeed have had a positive impact on surrounding property values.[10]

Palmer Square Apartments also caught the attention of influential leaders in the housing finance industry. The developers opened the buildings on a regular basis to tour groups even while rehabilitation was in progress. One of these tours was led by Anita Miller, a member of the Federal Home Loan Bank Board which regulates the savings and loan industry. She lauded the development as a "model for the industry"--for the three-way collaboration between a lending institution, a local development corporation and government. Miller further recommended that RESCORP establish a liaison with the Federal Home Loan Bank Board in Washington so that the FHLB would encourage similar housing undertakings by savings and loan associations in other cities around the nation.[11]

Reflections of the Developers

Six years after completion of the Palmer Square Apartments, Saul Klibanow of RESCORP and Paul Roldan of Hispanic Housing were well satisfied with their accomplishment. RESCORP had sought to rehabilitate a large number of apartments in a decaying community so that the decline could be reversed. Hispanic Housing had wanted to provide better housing for low-income Hispanics and to learn the development process through this experience. Both objectives had been achieved.

In reflecting on their experience the developers stressed that even though the Palmer Square Apartments development cost was substantially more expensive than the price of the usual cut-rate rehabilitation, the additional cost was necessary to assure the quality crucial to upgrading the community's self perception. They dared not risk failure because the buildings were to become the cornerstone of a reviving community.[12] On the other hand, Roldan points out, such massive rehabilitation is no longer feasible. With the type of financing now available, buildings must be in better condition, and tenants must enjoy higher incomes.

One of the developers' regrets was that the development was not on a larger scale of 200 to 300 units. Klibanow especially was concerned with scale and still laments the Illinois Housing

Development Authority's insistence that two of the eight original buildings be demolished.[13] However, both Klibanow and Roldan were satisfied that the 160-unit size turned out to be sufficient, although barely so, to make the kind of impact they had sought.

As a result of this experience both RESCORP and Hispanic Housing, in separate ways, proceeded with confidence to rehabilitate additional inner-city buildings, but on a larger scale. Their experience with Palmer Square Apartments reassured them that older buildings held up extremely well under substantial rehabilitation. Since then, Hispanic Housing has newly built or rehabilitated an additional 513 units of housing for families and elderly, not only in the Logan Square community but also in such Hispanic communities as Pilsen, Little Village and Humboldt Park. RESCORP moved forward to undertake a massive $25 million, 446-unit, multi-family rehabilitation in Chicago's South Shore community.

NOTES

1. Sally Levin, "Palmer Square Apartments: Neighborhood Threat Becomes Incentive," *Logan Square Free Press* (September 1979).

2. Ron Grossman, "Inner-city, ethnic groups take neighborhood revival into their own hands," *Chicago Tribune* (November 3, 1984), Section 3, p.1.

3. Saul Klibanow and Hipolito Roldan, interview February 4, 1986.

4. Sally Levin, p.12.

5. "Displacement Deterred," *Chicago Rehab Network Newsletter* (Dcember/January 1980), p.5.

6. Saul Klibanow and Hipolito Roldan.

7. *Chicago Rehab Network Newsletter*.

8. Saul Klibanow and Hipolito Roldan.

9. Ron Grossman.

10. Elizabeth Warren, Robert M. Aduddell and Raymond Tatalovich, *The Impact of Subsidized Housing on Property Values: A Two-Pronged Analysis of Chicago and Cook County Suburbs* (Chicago: Center for Urban Policy at Loyola University, 1983), pp.viii, xiii and 91.

11. "Earmarks of Success?," *RESCORP Newsletter* (February 1980), Volume 8, No.1.

12. Saul Klibanow and Hipolito Roldan.

13. Saul Klibanow and Hipolito Roldan.

8

'Specs' for Success:
A Summary

In each of the preceding case studies, the developers had to overcome both predictable and unforeseeable obstacles to make the housing more affordable for lower-income families and to reverse the neighborhood's decline. In several cases, they used innovative financing vehicles to produce more affordable housing. As not-for-profit sponsors of housing, they benefited from special grants and subsidies. As community-based housing developers, they enjoyed enough neighborhood support to allay resident fears about displacement and thus avoid costly delays or time-consuming protests.

In all six studies, the not-for-profits' leaders were not only dogged but enterprising as well. For example, they found keys to locked fiscal doors or avoided bankruptcy by trimming expenses which unsuccessful housing developers had not been able to do. The wedding of a not-for-profit developer with a for-profit contractor balanced off the strengths and weaknesses of each. A for-profit housing partner, for example, absorbed some costs as a tax advantage. The high cost of building maintenance often sinks a housing development. However, superior construction that needs less upkeep and greater tenant responsibility eases mortgage payments. Maintenance personnel who are all-around mechanics provide another economic advantage. They are an alternative to contracting out every repair job--when windows or sashes are broken, toilets clogged, sewers backed up or electrical systems overloaded.

The following summary of "tips" from not-for-profit developers relies, in the main, on a sponsor's own perception of mistakes made and corrected, obstacles encountered and overcome, or initiatives taken and their consequences. In the course of building new housing or rehabilitating deteriorated properties, the not-for-profit sponsor, usually without experience in housing, learned a great deal about the hazards of developing real estate. An experienced developer, on the other hand, might have already learned these lessons. They are recounted here for four reasons:

• to enable the housing industry and government housing agencies to understand better the unique experience of community-based, not-for-profit organizations when they try to produce more affordable housing for their neighborhood;

• to encourage churches and other community-based groups to explore whether they can play a role in neighborhood revitalization as sponsors of housing;

• to alert potential not-for-profit sponsors to the roadblocks they are likely to encounter and to suggest ways of overcoming them; and

• to persuade the framers of government policy, in Washington and elsewhere, to fashion a role for federal, state, county and municipal bodies in encouraging and supporting community development corporations whose aim is to produce more housing for families with low and middle incomes.

These tips are grouped together under nine headings: tenants, market, financing, community, design, structure, labor, ownership and mentors. Given the social concern of not-for-profit housing sponsors, it is not surprising that most tips have to do with the developer's relations with tenants. Since the sponsors were community-based institutions, their concern for neighborhood revitalization is evident in their interest in reviving the local housing market.

Tenants

1. Careful selection of tenants is crucial in the successful management of a lower-income development.

2. Where the social environment is blighted because of street

crime and a high degree of commercial and residential deterioration, the new housing "enclave" can survive and even thrive if tenants are willing to cooperate with each other and with management to stave off exterior threats.

3. Not-for-profit developers who have social goals in mind must understand the practical limitations of brick-and-mortar development and the danger of overburdening the development financially by generating resident expectations which cannot be realized.

4. Low-income households can become trustworthy tenants and social assets to the housing development, when screening is done painstakingly.

5. A highly involved management style, where the manager knows the tenants personally and establishes face-to-face relationships with each member of the household, is effective in maintaining the social controls necessary for a successful housing development. Interviewing children as well as adults helps to ensure a sense of neighborly responsibility.

6. A shared ideal, such as harmony amidst racial and economic diversity, can attract good tenants to a housing development.

7. The maintenance of a racial balance, to avoid a tipping point, is especially important in a housing development which rents simultaneously to subsidized and market-rate tenants and which is located in a neighborhood that has suffered substantial deterioration.

8. The early involvement of future residents improves the development's chances of success. By bringing into the planning process and onto the board of directors, people from the various income groups, a not-for-profit housing sponsor nurtures a special sense of community.

9. In larger developments, the use of full-time and professional staff for relocation and screening can prevent controversy, avoid legal suits and deflect community hostility.

10. Tenants willing and able to pay market-rate rents can be attracted to a housing development that is racially and economi-

cally integrated, even when the housing is next door to a notorious public housing project. They can be attracted by superior amenities, convenient location, reassuring around-the-clock security, and professional marketing.

Market

11. Visual evidence of high quality is needed to change local and downtown perceptions that the area is improving.

12. Housing stock of top quality at affordable prices can attract upwardly mobile households, who have previously moved out, back to a neighborhood that enjoys an ethnic identity of its own.

13. A not-for-profit developer, entering a local housing market that is no longer attracting private investment, can, given the right conditions, dramatically reverse the market's direction through large-scale, strategically located rehabilitation.

14. Upgrading a large number of the worst buildings in a neighborhood, all at once, can sometimes revive a declining community and radically alter the psychology of a depressed housing market.

15. Subsidized housing can have a benign and even a positive impact on the value of nearby property, when built or rehabbed with sensitivity to scale and quality.

Financing

16. Sweat equity enables some cash-poor buyers to assemble the down payment they need to buy the housing in which they will live.

17. Limiting the equity of a cooperative owner in a housing development may be effective in keeping housing affordable for lower-income households as real estate values rise.

18. Using large down payments as working capital can reduce the cost of financing the initial construction.

19. Using large down payments as working capital can leverage financing from traditional lending institutions.

Community

20. The rehabilitation of existing housing in inner-city neighborhoods is expedited when the developer responds to the real or perceived needs or fears of the surrounding community, thus averting local opposition.With a concern for existing tenants, rehabilitation can proceed without major conflicts over relocation.

21. The appearance of not-for-profit sponsors of housing has frequently prompted a change of neighborhood strategy with regard to vacant, boarded-up apartment buildings. Previously, when such a building was abandoned by its owners and brought to housing court, the local block club would demand its immediate demolition. Now another alternative is possible: the preservation of a sound but vacant structure by rehabilitating it. Increasingly, local citizens' groups mute their demand for demolition and instead search for a community-based institution--whether for-profit or not-for-profit--to buy and rehab the multi-apartment building. Saving the building is now seen as an act of neighborhood revitalization. Additional apartments become available for neighbors and a vacant lot with a potential for accumulating rubbish and abandoned autos is avoided.

Design

22. The central atrium feature of a high rise nurtures a sense of community and security.

23. The architectural principles of "defensible space" persuade potential renters that a housing development is a safe "enclave" in an otherwise dangerous urban environment.

Structure

24. Liveability is enhanced and community acceptance made easier when families with children are housed only in low-rise buildings.

25. To reduce construction costs and subsequent maintenance, pre-cast concrete and modular construction can be utilized.

26. The basic structure of old, deteriorating buildings in the inner city is generally sound enough to sustain "life extension" rehabilitation, thus enabling lenders to make mortgage loans for

terms of thirty to forty years.

27. Once a housing development has been completed, its success is often jeopardized by the absence of tight controls over operating expenses, especially when tasks and responsibilities are contracted out that could have been undertaken in-house.

Labor

28. Under the right conditions, sweat equity can marginally reduce the cost of construction. When sweat equity labor is utilized, additional time, patience and effort is demanded of both the developer and the contractor.

Ownership

29. A housing cooperative for lower-income households is more likely to succeed when it enjoys the initial leadership and support of a stable sponsor.

Land

30. The final cost of a housing development can be significantly reduced by purchasing surplus, government-owned properties which stand vacant and which nobody else wants.

Mentors

31. Mentors play crucial roles in guiding novice developers of not-for-profit housing to plan, begin and complete the development process.

* * * *

The six case studies presented here are a tribute to the not-for-profit developer's remarkable mix of initiative, flexibility, imagination and doggedness. They each succeeded in producing their final product: desirable housing at lower-than-market prices. Each helped reverse the direction of a declining community.

Index